A note to the 21st century reader...

We have endeavoured to reproduce in readable form the exact content of John Gadbury's text first published in London in 1659. At this time academic books were increasingly being published in English rather than Latin and although Gadbury uses several Latin phrases amongst his discourse in the pages following, in most cases he follows up with a translation in straightforward English. Like Lilly in his *Christian Astrology* (1647) and Culpeper in his *Herbal* (1653) Gadbury does not assume that all his readers are closeted scholars; he wishes to reach all who can read and write.

English as a written language took great strides after the publication of the King James Bible in 1611 but Samuel Johnson's famous dictionary was over a hundred years in the future and the spellings of many words were far from standardised. Gadbury spells the word 'year' for instance as both 'year' and 'yeer' in different parts of this book. In this and several other instances we have simply followed him, preserving the quaint spellings like 'ecliptique', 'signifie', 'Dragon's Tayl' etc. where the phonetic meaning is obvious. Only in certain parts of the text where a passage is not immediately clear have we changed any words into modern English. All else, apart from his notes in the margins (which have not been included), is as he wrote it. Where he speaks of a 'revolution' chart, of which there are several examples referring to King Charles, he means the Sun's revolution (*revolutio Solis*) or what we would today call a Solar Return.

In the original manuscript Gadbury sometimes used aspect and planetary symbols instead of words in his sentences, but in this he wasn't consistent and we have put everything into words for the sake of clarity. Above all we have attempted to preserve the fluidity, experimental form and particularly the spirit of the colourful prose of the seventeenth century.

Published in 2011 by
The Wessex Astrologer
4A Woodside Road
Bournemouth
BH5 2AZ
www.wessexastrologer.com

Re-typeset from the Ascella 2003 facsimile version
Nativity of the Late King Charles, 1659.
© The Wessex Astrologer 2011
All rights reserved

ISBN 9781902405513

A catalogue record of this book is available at The British Library

Cover design by Tania at Creative Byte, Poole, Dorset

The
NATIVITY
of the late
King CHARLS

Astrologically and faithfully performed;

with

REASONS IN ART,
Of the various success and misfortune
of
His whole LIFE.

Being (occasionally) a brief History of our late unhappy
WARS.

Unto which is added (by way of APPENDIX)
the Genitures of the late Queen, Prince, etc.,
And their sympathy, or antipathy with this illustrious
Nativity compared.

By John Gadbury,

Printed by James Cottrel, London, August, 1659.

The Epistle Dedicatory.

To the most worthily Accomplished, my true approved Friend,

Mr. THO. BARTON,
of
LONDON,
Merchant.

Most worthy Sir!
The grateful river doth then demonstrate itself to be such, when it willingly rendereth its juster tribute to the sea. And were not your frequent favours and friendships so many, and so highly obliging; yet, your exquisite skill in Coelestial Knowledge (a thing perfectly prodigious to vulgar pates!) might very well challenge (as due) a far greater respect from me, than the dedication of these few sheets of paper.

    The subject of this little book may seem strange to such persons that know nothing above the earth they tread on. Yet to you (worthy Sir!) being acquainted with the radix thereof, it cannot but appear otherwise.

    While I travailed with this diminutive tract, you were (by consent) designed its foster father; and now it is come to a perfect birth, it is my chiefest ambition to entitle it unto your worthy tuition and patronage.

    Honoured Sir! The certain and continued knowledge I have had of your humanity and gentle nature, prevents me of all apologies, and makes me (not a little) proud of this convenient opportunity to testifie to the world how much I am,

    And am also willing to continue,
        Worthy Sir!
        Your Humble Servant
        and
        True Honourer,

John Gadbury

To the Noble
STUDENTS in ART,
And all other Impartial
READERS.

Gentlemen!
The nativity I here present you with is most eminent and remarkable, as was the unfortunate person unto whom it belonged. And Astrologie from all the genitures of princes (published) will hardly receive more ample demonstration. For not one accident of moment (either of good or bad consequence) hath happened to this princely native throughout the whole course of his life but an apparent reason thereof is to be found in his nativity; as is sufficiently evidenced (I presume) in the following discourse.

I know it is accounted a curiosity of the first magnitude to intermeddle with the genitures of princes. And am not ignorant that by the greatest politicians and our chief masters in Astrologie, we are prohibited such inspections. The politician takes cognizance of the great dangers and eminent disadvantages the making known a Prince's destiny may do him. Astrologers acquaint us with the unhappy prejudice those usually plunge themselves into, that undertake to be too plaine with a Prince in anything, but more especially his fate, if so be that it chance to be evil.

But should we admit of both their reasons to be convincing and undeniable, (which I cannot in reason wholly assent unto, for I account it every whit as useful and necessary for an artist to acquaint a prince with the truth, though it concern his ill, as a peasant); yet without doubt an artist may lawfully make observations on the scheme of a prince's birth after his expiration, and never incur the guilt of high treason or the censure of an ingenuous artist. It being more than probable that (then) nothing of treachery or baseness can be acted under pretence thereof, either to the detriment of his person or attempts.

And the reason (if I may be bold to deliver my opinion) of those interdictions, was the parasitical practise of some Astrologers, who, being little acquainted with art (and less with honesty), used to tickle the ears of great persons with golden predictions, that themselves might have the more glorious reward; and this under pretence of calculating their nativities. Whence Astrologie hath been as little (if not less) beholden to them as unto its most publique and professed enemies. For so full of flatteries and forgeries have most of their presages been, only to delight the fancies of their deluded clients, that instead of doing them service they have only spread a more dangerous snare in their way. Which treacherous practise caused the learned Tacitus to conclude them (in the general, as – unjustly – believing all alike): *Genus hominum, insidum principibus*, i.e. 'a company of fellowes always perfidious to princes'. And indeed from the same ground have divers other learned persons accounted Astrologie a most ridiculous and vain thing; only a higher degree of *liedger-de-maine* (as it pretendeth to treat of the stars) and Astrologers themselves but a crew of liberal juglers.

Nevertheless Astrologie, *quatenus* Astrologie, excelleth all other arts and sciences. Howbeit, by reason of the ignorance and imposture of some that profess it, and the too hasty determination of others that rashly censure it, it is become the most inferiour (if not the contempt and scorn) of all others. And now it is no wonder for your freshmen and junior sophists at Oxford and Cambridge, to bawl aloud in the schools – *Astrologia non est Scientia*! And is not Astrologie admirably defended in the mean time? What would the lazy and ignorant professors thereof have done had not the learned Sir Christopher Heydon, above half a century of years since, wrote a defence thereof? Astrology is now assaulted on every side, and our greatest pretenders do homage to Harpocrates (the god of silence), as if they were nothing at all concerned. We think we do a great service for the art if, in an almanac, we (like the Scythian beast) squirt out some filth in the faces of our pursuers! When alas, in the meantime, most book-sellers' shops swarm with big-belly'd treatises against Astrologie, and those like to remain to posterity unanswered.

But to return: (such is the property of things evil), the seed of this pernicious and art-destroying villany hath not only thriven but grown to a very great and spreading tree among us, which hath almost choaked and stifled the verity of this science! Many pretenders shrowding themselves under the branches thereof, professing great skill in conjuration, necromancie, theurgiee, the crystal, and what not? – when not one in ten of them knows what a nativity means. Talk to them of their genius, a sigil, lamen, charm, love-powder etc., they are then in their element, and Ptolemy himself may be accounted too weak a disputant for them. But question with them concerning art, or any thing worthy, and from a plowman you may receive as much true satisfaction. I could (with ease) point at some by name, (and those that the world esteems of otherwise), did I not believe I should rather do disservice to the fair Urania, than thereby any wayes advantage her cause. For such considents (like rapid torrents) swell and foam the more, and shew the greater fury for the meeting a damn in their violence.

The true Astrologer abominates all such gypsie-like shifts, as much as a Reverend Divine, a spittle pulpit. He goes not beyond the line of his art, but where he meets with any thing in his practise not exactly agreeing with the literal sense of his rules or aphorisms, intermixes reason therewith (not any of the fooleries before mentioned) and thereby frees his science from scandal, and corrects the unbelief of his adversary. And really it is not for every man to hope to be an Astrologer; for heaven clubs to the act of his creation in a especial manner! An artist (as a poet) is born, not made.

I see not (I seriously profess) but if Astrology were sedulously observed, its maximes and problems at length might be found as perfect and certain as Euclid's. In former dayes, when the art could boast of nothing nigh such perfection as now, it was accounted no wonder for a genethliaque to predict things concerning men *ad mensem*; yea, sometimes *ad diem*. But now, as if the excellency, worth and truth of Astrology run retrograde, it is little less than a miracle to be done *ad annum*. (Yea, the practise and writings of some would easily induce us to believe that it is impossible to be performed at all!)

Spurina forewarned Caesar of the Ides of March. Junctine, a Florentine, foresaw his death to a day. Zonarus reports that an artist (being informed of Julian his being engaged with his army to fight his enemies) read these words in the heavens: *hodie Julianus in Persia occiditur*. 'Today is Julian slain in Persia'! And certainly, if errours at any time happen in the calculating or judging nativities, 'tis: *non ex Scientiae imbecillitate, sed professorum*. – 'Not from any incertaintie or weakness of the art, but from the knavery, negligence, or want of skill in the persons professing it'.

I could wish that students in this art were more serious in their observations, and more rational and wary in their determinations. By such means Astrology should not need the stamp of Caesar to protect it, or to make it currant; for by its own merit and innate worth it would shine and dilate its beneficial rayes as the noon-tide sun, and appear as honourable among the arts as Apollo among the Muses. And that the modest and indulgent student may not want a certain and verified example of a nativity, have I been at the ensuing pains in this illustrious geniture; it being but the forerunner of a book more considerable, which I am at the present employed about, wherein I shall (God permitting life) present the lovers of science with two hundred (at the least) verified nativities, the one half thereof being of persons yet living. And this I undertake, to detect the ignorance of some professing art, and to acquaint the adversaries, that Astrologie is not so barren a science but that the true Astrologer may thereby inform any native of the most remarkable and occult accidents that can naturally attend him.

Many (I know) will inspect this tractate as much for the person's sake whose nativity it was, as for the respect they have to art. I matter not upon what account it be perus'd; so that Astrologie receive its just due, I am satisfied; for to that purpose I write it, and in hopes of accomplishing that end I shall continue serviceable to the true sons of art, while I am,

John Gadbury

From my house neer *Strand* bridge without *Temple Bar*,
February 5, 1658.

An Advertisement

Hartgil's Tables of the fixed Stars, reduced to this our Age:
It is a book useful in nativities, questions, navigation etc. And sold by the Company of Stationers.

The Seamans Guide;
a book of singular use, written by Timothy Gadbury and sold by Francis Cossinet at the 'Anchor and Mariner' in Tower Street.

The Doctrine of Nativities,
explaining the whole art of directions and revolutions, together with tables for calculating the planets places for any time past, present or to come; with the *Doctrine of Horary Questions* by way of Appendix added thereunto. By John Gadbury, the author of this book; sold by William Larnar, Giles Calvert and Daniel White, at their shops in St Paul's churchyard and on Ludgate Hill.

That most excellent and unanswerable
Defence of Judicial Astrologie,
wrote against Mr Chambers neer sixty yeers since, by that eminently learned knight, Sir Christopher Heydon, is by reason of its excellent use and worth now re-printing by Joseph Moxon, at the sign of 'Atlas' in Cornhill, where globes of all sizes, and the Mathematical Jewel, are also sold.

THE
NATIVITIE
of
CHARLS STUART

late King of England, Scotland,
Ireland etc.
Astrologically handled.

K ing Charls, the most unfortunate of Princes, was born at Dumferlin in Scotland, in the yeer of our Lord God, 1600, on November the 19th, 10 hours 2 minutes 35 seconds, P.M. The latitude of which place is 56 degrees North, and the planets places at that time are found to be thus – both in longitude and latitude.

Long Planet
Sun 08 Sag 02
Saturn 06 Scorpio 08
Jupiter 19 Virgo 15
Mars 26 Sag 10
Venus 22 Sag 15
Mercury 09 Sag 38
Moon 04 Libra 30
N.Node 14 Virgo 28

Lat Planet

Saturn 02 06 N.A.
Jupiter 01 01 N.A.
Mars 00 12 S.D.
Venus 00 29 S.D.
Mercury 00 56 S.D.
Moon 05 03 S.A.

Nativity of the Late King Charles

Now to erect the figure of this nativity, I do thus:

	d.	m.
Longitude of Sun is Sagittarius	8	2
His Right Ascention is	246	15
The R.A. of time is	150	39
Both added together	396	54
Subtract	360	
Then the A.R. M.C. is	36	54
add	30	
Asc. Obl. Dom. undec.	66	54
add	30	
Asc. Obl. Dom. Duodec.	96	54
add	30	
Asc. Obl. Ascend.	126	54
Add	30	
Asc. Obl. Dom. Secund.	156	54
add	30	
Asc. Obl. Dom. Tert.	186	54

Thus the right and oblique ascentions of the six houses to the orient are obtained. And because my *Doctrine of Nativities* is not in the hands of every man, the price thereof being as considerable as its bulk or bigness, I shall here set the figure of this nativitie artificially, for the advantage and use of those that have not seen that book.

The elevation of the Pole at Dumferling in Scotland is 56 degrees and the circles of position of the other houses are as followeth:

The elevation of the 11th and 3rd houses	36° 33'
The elevation of the 12th and 2nd houses	52° 5'

Now you are to understand that the Midheaven, or tenth house, is a standing circle of position of itself, and as the five cases in grammar decline or fall from the *nominative*, which is *rectus casus*; so the other five houses decline or fall from the *Medium Coeli*, that being a right sphear, and therefore can admit of no obliquity.

Nativity of the Late King Charles

For to finde the degrees and minutes of the Ecliptique, agreeing to the ascentions of the respective houses, under the several elevations before mentioned, I do thus:

Pro Cuspide X. Ascentio recta, M.C. est 36° 54'

	d.	m.	Taurus d.		m.
Proxime Major	37	34	10	36	54
Proxime Minor	36	36	9	36	36
Different	0	58	1	0	18

Then I say by the logistical logarithms, if 58.m. give 60, what is 18.m?

18m.	0		947712	
58	0		998528	subtract
17	25		946244	

Hence, *vera cuspis* M.C. *est* Taurus 9° 17' 25"

Pro Cuspide XI. Asc. 66° 54'. lat. 36° 33'

Lat. 36 Proxime Major	67	16	Gemini 26	66	54
Lat. 36 Proxime Minor	66	13	Gemini 25	66	13
Different	1	3	Gemini 1		41

If 63m. give 60m. what 41m?

0° 41'			983463	
1 3			1002120	subtract
0 39	10.		981343	

Ergo, cuspis XI. *in lat.* 36° *est* Gemini 25° 39' 10".

	d.	m.	Gemini d.		m.
Lat.37. proxime Major	67	38	27	66	54
Lat.37. proxime Minor	66	34	26	66	34
Different.	1	4	1		20

Nativity of the Late King Charles

If 64 m. gives 60 m. what 20 m?
    0° 20'   952287
    1   4   1002804 subtract
    ―――――――――――――
    0 18. 45.   949483

Ergo, cuspis XI. *in lat.* 37 *est* Gemini 26° 18' 45".
    Different. *Cusp. lat.* 36/37 *est* 0° 39' 35".

Then I say, if 60m. give 39m. 35 sec. what 33 m?
    39' 35"   987936
    33' 0   974036 add
    ――――――――――――
    24 55   961972

Which added to Gemini 25° 39' 10" leaves the true cusp of the eleventh house in latit. of 16° 33', Gemini 26° 4' 5".

Pro Cusp. 12. Ascent. 36° 54'. Lat. 52° 5'.

Lat. 52° 'tis just in Leo 2° 0' without equation.

	d.	m.	Leo	d.	m.
Lat. 53. Proxime Major	97	13	3	96	54
Lat. 53 Proxime Minor	95	48	2	95	48
	1	25	1	1	6

    If 85m. give 60m. what 66m?
    1   6   825661
    1   25   837311 subtract
    ――――――――――――――
    46' 15"   988350

Ergo, cuspis XII. *in lat.* 53. *est* Leo 2° 46' 15".
    Differentia cusp. lat. 52/53 est 46' 15".

Then I say, if 60m. gives 46m. 15sec. what 5 min?
    46'   15   988696
    5   0   892082 add
    ――――――――――――
    3   55   880778

Nativity of the Late King Charles

Which added to Leo 2 degrees, leaves the true cusp of the twelfth house in the latitude of 52° 5' in Leo 2° 3' 55".

Pro Cuspis 1. Ascen. 126° 54' lat. 56°.

	d	m	Leo	d	m
Proxime Major	126	55	25	126	54
Proxime Minor	125	24	24	125	24
Different.	1	31	1	1	30

If 91m. give 60m. what 90 m?

1	30	839794
1	31	840280 subtract
59'	20"	999514

Ergo, vera cuspis Ascend. est Leo 24° 59' 20".

Pro Cuspide 2. Ascent. 156° 54' Lat. 52° 5'.

	d	m	Virgo	d	m
Lat 52. Proxime Major	157	8	14	156	54
Lat 52. Proxime Minor	155	42	13	155	42
Different.	1	26	1	12	12

If 86m. gives 60m. what 72 m?

1	12	829732
1	26	837311 subtract
50'	10"	992421

Cuspis 2. Lat. 52° est Virgo 13° 50' 10".

	d	m	Virgo	d	m
Lat. 53. Proxime Major	158	7	15	156	54
Lat. 53. Proxime Minor	156	50	14	156	50
Different.	1	17	1	0	4

Nativity of the Late King Charles

If 77m. give 60m. what 4m?

0	4	714267
1	17	833277 subtract
3'	50"	880990

Ergo, cuspis 2 Lat. 53 *est* Virgo 14° 3' 50".
Different. cusp. Lat. 52/53 est 12' 40".

If 60m. give 12m. 40sec. what 5m?

12	40	932451
5	0	892082 add
1'	5"	824533

Which being added to Virgo 13° 50' 10" leaves the true cusp of the second in Virgo 13° 51' 15".

Pro Cusp. 3. Ascent. 186° 54'. Lat. 36° 33'.

	d.	m.	Libra	d.	m.
Lat. 36. Proxime Major	187	14	6	186	54
Lat 36. Proxime Minor	186	2	5	186	2
Different.	1	12	1	0	52

If 72m. gives 60m. what 52m?

0°	52'	784164
1	12	829779 subtract
0 m.	50 sec.	814385

Cuspis 3 *in Lat.* 36 *est* Libra 5° 0' 50".

	d.	m.	Libra	d.	m.
Lat. 37. Proxime Major	187	18	6	186	54
Lat. 37 Proxime Minor	186	5	5	186	5
	1	13	1	0	49

If 75 min. gives 60 min. what 49 min?

Nativity of the Late King Charles

0°	49'	814267
1	13	829779 subtract
41 m.	54 sec.	984488

Ergo cuspis 3. in Lat. 37. est Libra 5° 41' 54".
Differentia cusp. Lat. 36/37 est 41' 4".

If 60m. give 41m. 4sec. what 33m?

41	4	983551
33	0	974036 adde.
22	35 sec.	957587

Vera cuspis 3. est Libra 5° 22' 35".

Collectio cuspidum

	S	D	M	Sec		S	D	M	Sec
10	♉	9	17	25	4	♏	9	17	25
11	♊	26	4	5	5	♐	26	4	5
12	♌	2	3	55	6	♒	2	3	55
1	♌	24	59	20	7	♒	24	59	20
2	♍	13	51	15	8	♓	13	51	15
3	♎	5	22	35	9	♈	5	22	35

The opposite houses have opposite signs, degrees etc.

Next I shall present you with an epitomie of the whole calculation.

Nativity of the Late King Charles

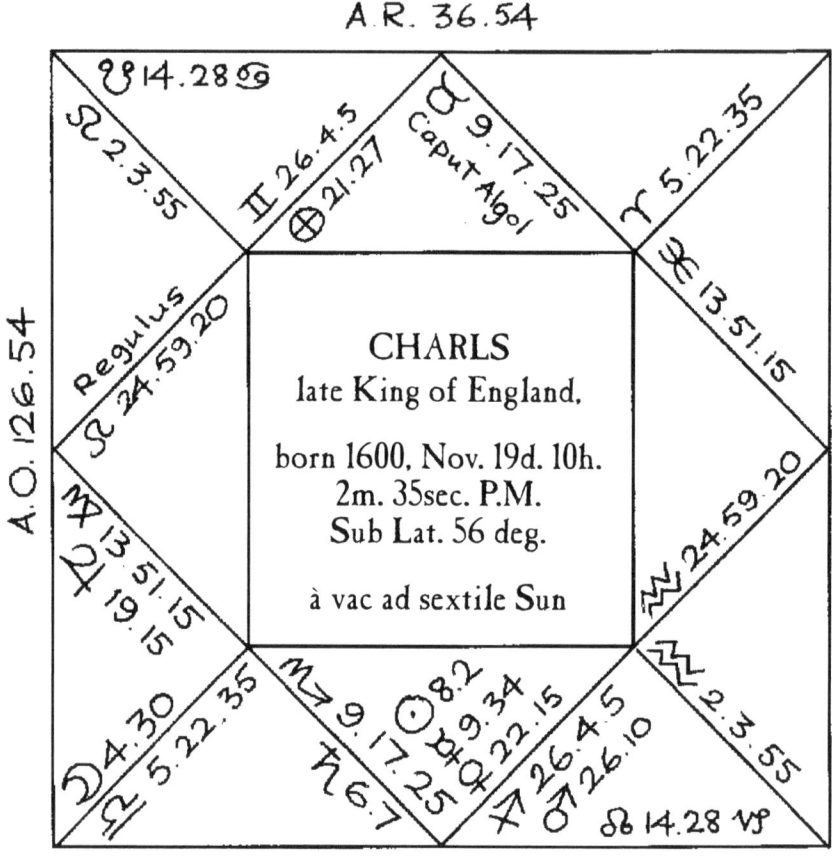

The *fortitudes* of the planets in this figure, their *debilities* being deducted, are as follows:

$$\begin{bmatrix} \odot \\ \hbar \\ 4 \\ \sigma \\ \varphi \\ \varrho \\ \mathcal{D} \end{bmatrix} \text{ is strong by } \begin{bmatrix} 1 \\ 12 \\ 6 \\ 14 \\ 11 \\ 3 \\ 3 \end{bmatrix} \text{ testimonies}$$

The Antiscions and Contra-antiscions of the PLANETS.

Antiscion	S	D	M	Contra-Antiscion	S	D	M
♄	♉	23	52	♄	♏	23	52
♃	♈	10	45	♃	♎	10	45
♂	♑	3	50	♂	♋	3	50
☉	♑	21	58	☉	♋	21	58
♀	♑	7	45	♀	♋	7	45
☿	♑	20	26	☿	♋	20	26
☽	♓	25	30	☽	♍	25	30

A Speculum for this Nativity.

Planets	D.D.	♈	♉	♊	♋	♌	♍	♎	♏	♐	♑	♒	♓
	1.16												
	2.17												
	3.18												
☽ 4.30 ♃ 19.15	4.19	☍	△	△ □	□ ✶	✶	♃	☽	✶	✶ □	□ △	△	☍
	5.20												
♄ 6.7	6.21		☍	⊕	△	□	✶		♄		✶	□	△
♀ 22.15	7.22	□	△		☍		△	□	✶		♀		✶
☉ 8.2	8.23	□	△		☍		△	□	✶		☉		✶
☿ 9.34	9.24	□	MC △		☍		△	□	✶		☿		✶
	10.25					ASC							
♂ 26.10	11.26	□	△		☍		△	□	✶		♂		✶
	12.27												
	13.28												
☊ 14.28	14.29				☋						☊		
	15.30												

Nativity of the Late King Charles

A Speculum of the Directions belonging to this Nativity.

	Anno Christ	Ascen.	Midhvn.	Sun	Moon	P.Fortuna
0	1600					
1	1601			☌ ☿ 34		
2	1602					
3	1603					T. ♂ 41
4	1604				✶ ☉ ☍	
5	1605		T. ♃ 37	T. ☿ 55	✶ ☿ 16	☍ ♂ 55
6	1606					
7	1607	T. ☿ 39			CA ⎱ ♃ 42 T ⎰	
8	1608					
9	1609		△ ♃ 53			T. ♂ 3
10	1610					
11	1611			T. ♄ 20 □ ♃ 17		
12	1612		T. ♄ 40			
13	1613					
14	1614		A. ♄ 42	☌ ♀ 25		CA ♂ ⎱ 2 □ ☽ ⎰
15	1615					△ ♄ ⎱ 52 T. ♃ ⎰
16	1616		T. ♂ 46			
17	1617	✶ ♄ 0		T. ♂ 20	T. ☿ 24	CA. ♀ 59
18	1618	T. ♀ 19		☌ ♂ 35		
19	1619	□ ☉ 54				
20	1620		T. ☿ 54			
21	1621				✶ ♀ 26	
22	1622	□ ☿ 20		T. ♀ 44		
23	1623				T. ♂ 29	T. ☿ 45

A Speculum of the Directions belonging to this Nativity.

24	1624					
25	1625		△☽ 37			ad ☋ 27
26	1626				⚹ ♂ 11	
27	1627	T. ♃ 26		□ ☽ A ♂ } 41		
28	1628		T. ♃ 15			
29	1629		☍ ☉ 21	T. ☿ 21 ⚹ ♄ 30		
30	1630		☍ ☿ 54 cum lat.		T. ♂ 50	
31	1631		☍ ☿ 4 sine lat.	A. ♀ 35		⚹ ♃ 6
32	1632					T. ♀ CA ☿ } 0
33	1633					
34	1634					CA ☉ 23
35	1635	☌ ♃ 35 cum lat.	T. ♀ 44			
36	1636	☌ ♃ 53 sine lat.		T. ♃ 6		
37	1637				☌ ♄ 37 cum lat.	
38	1638			ad ☊ 52	☌ ♄ 23 cum lat.	
39	1639					
40	1640					T. ♄ 24
41	1641	□ ♀ 25	□ ♃ 24			
42	1642					
43	1643		T. ♄ 18 ⊕ 48			
44	1644	T. ♂ 4	☍ ♀ 39	T. ♂ 4 △ ♃ 20		T. ♄ 3
45	1645			A. ☿ 13		
46	1646	CA ☽ 19				
47	1647	□ ♂ 20	T. ♂ 39	A. ☉ 31		
48	1648				T. ♀ 3	

Nativity of the Late King Charles

The Circles of Position of the Sun, Moon, and Part of Fortune were thus obtained.

1. Of the Sun.

Longit. Sun est Sagittarius	8° 2'.
Declin. Merid. Sub. Ter.	21.43
Ascentio Recta	246.15
Ascentio Recta I.C.	216.54
Distant. a I.C.	29.21
Circulus Positionis	25°
Descent. Obliq. Sun	55.34

2. Of the Moon.

Longit. Moon est Libra	4.30
Latitud. Moon	5.3
Declin. Merid. Sub. Ter.	6.23
Ascentio Recta	184.8
Ascentio Recta I.C.	216.54
Distant. a I.C.	32.46
Circulus Positionis	36°
Ascen. Obliq.	185.34

3. Of Pars Fortuna

Longitud. Pars Fortuna est Gemini	21° 27'.
Declin. Merid. Sub. Ter.	23.15
Ascentio Recta	80.41
Ascentio Recta M.C.	36.54
Distant. a M.C.	43.47
Circulus Positionis	35°
Ascent. Obliqua.	63.13

The Midheaven and Ascendent are standing circles of position themselves, there is therefore no need of operating to finde them, then what before was done, in the setting of the figure. This done, I shall come in the next place to give a *general judgement* on this nativity, wherein I shall promise my reader to be as impartial, and carry as even a hand all along, as art and honesty in a geniture so weighty and considerable, will permit.

Nativity of the Late King Charles

A General Judgement on this Nativity.
Of the Horoscope or first House.

In this illustrious geniture there doth ascend the last decade of the fierie sign Leo; and the regal star Regulus, or heart of the Lyon, is *secundum longitudinem* directly horoscopical. The Sun, who is *Rex planetarum*, the principal of all the planets, is Lord of the Ascendant, and in Sagittarius a kingly sign, the joy and delight of the benign planet Jupiter. He is also in corporal conjunction of Mercury, and neer unto the body of Mars and Venus, both which planets cast a friendly aspect to the Ascendant; and besides these, the Luminaries are in sextile to each other, the Moon being in Libra, which is of Astrologers termed *signum justitiae*, or the sign of justice, and therefore not the least to be considered.

All which testimonies do astrologically demonstrate the temperature of this native to be sanguine cholerique; which humors prevailing argued him to be of disposition and behavior courteous and affable, yet princelike, magnanimous and imperious. The Sun, as he is *Dominus Ascendentis* is, by being in conjunction with Mercury, the proper and peculiar significator of manners; and being posited in Sagittarius, they declare him to have been a person of a valiant and heroick spirit, voyd of fear, and of minde and inclination both generous and lofty. See *Origanus de effectib. folio 595.* and my *Doctrine of Nativities, folio 97.*

The authors of the history of this Prince's life (for divers have been observators thereon, though none astrologically before myself to any purpose, that I know of) relate, that of himself he was a person as noble, magnanimous, and as well qualified a gentleman every way as any prince in the world could be. He was courteous and friendly to all persons generally; a man of great spirit, lofty, imperious, and desirous of honour. Yet so noble was he, and of so compassionate a spirit, that he abhorred and hated war and bloodshed; yea, he was so great an enemy thereunto (notwithstanding his sad fate was such as to be put to death for the very thing he most of all detested, and from his very heart hated) that he could never be gotten to seal a pardon to anyone condemned for murther, although he had been requested thereunto at any time by his nearest relations, and greatest favourites: as to instance in the case of Stamford, who had killed a man in Fleet Street, London, whose pardon the Duke of Buckingham implored from him, but by no means could obtain it.

The understanding of this native is known from the position of Mercury being in reception with Jupiter and sextile of the Moon, which presaged him to be a person of great prudence and ingenuity, of an excellent wit, and that both sharp and active, and in a greater measure than ordinary, in that Mercury is posited so neer the beams of Mars and Venus in Sagittarius. The consideration of which prevents my wonder at the ignorance (or malice rather) of some men, who (because cross fortune had sequestred his person and rendred him prisoner to those he sometimes by prerogative ruled) would indeavour to perswade the world he was of judgement but indifferent and easie, and that his understanding was under hatches also; and therefore envie him the being author of some most elegant and incomparably well-penn'd treatises. Whereas it is impossible for the wisest of mortals to pen a sorrow so to the life, as is that tragical story, except they had been partakers of the trouble, or sharers in the grief it expresseth. But leaving those sciolists to their contented slavery of judgement, I return...

In particular he was inclineable to learn arts and sciences and without question might very much affect both eloquence and oratory, and indeed all manner of praiseworthy knowledge; but although he might be affected with eloquence and oratory, yet should he have been subject to some kinde of defect therein, as is apparent, by the combustion of Mercury and his position under the earth; and of this opinion was the learned Cardan when he wrote – *Mercurius majorem habet vim ad artes infra terram, ad Eloquentiam Supra: Seg.7. Apho. 131.*

One of the observators on the actions of this native's life, gives this character of his understanding in his younger yeers:

> 'While he was young he followed his Book seriously, which his elder brother Prince Henry could not indure, and therefore King James would frequently blame Prince Henry with the neglect of his Book, and tell him how his brother Charls followed it. Whereupon Prince Henry would reply – when that he himself should be King, he would make his brother Charls Arch-Bishop of Canterbury.'

Of his understanding and judgement at riper yeers, the same author hath these words:

Nativity of the Late King Charles

'To speak truly of him, he had many singular good parts in nature; he was an excellent horsman, would shoot well at a mark, had singular skill in limning, a good mathematician, not unskilful in musique, well read in divinity, excellently in history; he had a quick and sharp conception, would write his minde singularly well and in good language. He would apprehend a matter in difference betwixt party and party with great readiness, and methodize a long matter, or contract it in few lines. Insomuch (saith this author) as I have heard Sir R.H. (Robert Holborn) oft say – He had a quicker conception, and would sooner understand a case in law, or with more sharpness drive the matter to the head, than any of his Privie Council.'

(Mr. L. *Monarchy*, page 75).

As Mercury is significator of the understanding, so he is patron of speech also, and by his being combust of the Sun neer many violent fixed stars, might very well denote an impediment or hindrance therein. But he being in an Angle, and a sign having voyce, namely Sagittarius, and therein sextile of the Moon and reception with Jupiter, demonstrates the impediment to be the less, and it shall very rarely be taken notice of, except the native happen to be moved by choler to speak in passion or hastily.

It is most true that he had an impediment in his speech, yet it was not so great but that at some times he would deliver himself as freely and articulately as any of the best orators in the world. As to instance in that rhetorical reply of his to the High Court of Justice on Saturday 20 January 1648, the first day he was brought before them to his tryal, when and where he spake without the least impediment or hinderance at all – As is recorded by Mr L. in *Monarchy* page 78, and averred by divers others, who there had the hap to hear him.

His person is described by the sign ascending, and the Lord thereof in Sagittarius, which argued it to be of a more than middle stature, strongly made, and very big upward; so big that (it is reported) when he intended his escape from the Isle of Wight, he got his whole body to the chest out of the window, and sticking thereat, was discovered, and so enforced back again. His head was somewhat large, hair of a brightish brown; his eyes large and of a quick and piercing sight, forehead very high and full; the visage oval, complexion mostly sanguine; an exact symmetry and proportion in all his members: he was both strong, valiant and active. Indeed there are no less then four of the seven planets in this nativity that have South latitude, and I remember it to be an aphorism of Ptolomie's – *Si latitudo Austrealis est, agiles erunt*. 'If the latitudes of the planets in a nativity happen to be South, the native will be active, quick and nimble'.

As the Ascendent and Lord thereof are free from the malignant beams of the Infortunes, and the ill aspects of the Lords of the sixth, eighth and fourth houses; they denote the native to be of a healthful, sound, vigorous, and firm constitution, and by consequence very free from diseases.

For the soundness of his constitution; that is known by the wonderful and admired activity he was wont to shew at all praiseworthy exercises and recreations, and by his being so seldom sick. And Mr W. Sanderson in his *History* reporteth, that a physitian being present at the dissection of his body relates – 'That nature had designed him above the most of mortal men for a long life'. But although this be a convincing argument of the vigor and strength of his constitution, yet I am not of that physitian's opinion in relation to life, for had nature ordained him for a longer life then he lived, without peradventure he had not then dyed. Most certain it is, that he who says to the sea, 'Hitherto shalt thou come, but no further; and here shall thy proud waves be stopped', doth also limit the life of man to such a certain time, beyond the bounds of which he cannot pass. Which very consideration moved an ingenious artist and good friend of mine (Mr. B.) upon occasion of some discourse of this nature, to say – 'That had not the unhappy difference between this Princely Native and his Parliament hapned, but he had first dissolved them; a Barons' War might have overtaken us, and so his impending fate should have been brought about without them.' And thus much for the judicials pertaining to the first house. I shall be briefer in the judgements belonging to the rest of the houses, forasmuch as they all depend upon the judgements of this, as is most excellently proved by that eminent artist, Johannes Baptista Morinus, late of France.

Judgements belonging to the Second House.

Jupiter in the second house is an assured argument of riches, and of a competencie of the goods of fortune. – *Jupiter enim in secunda, divitias*

Nativity of the Late King Charles

et omne genus felicitatis significat, faith *Cardan, cap.1. de jud. Gen.* and *Origanus, fol. 611. de effectib* maintains, That if the fortunate planets are posited in the second house, they endow the native with riches and much felicity; chiefly if Jupiter be there.

This according to the general position and signification of Jupiter there. But as there is no general that admits not of exception, we shall finde these rules and aphorisms liable to the same fate. For, if we consider Jupiter's location in Virgo, namely his detriment, and in square to Mars and Venus, and (platiquely) of Mercury and the Sun also, we shall then finde the aforesaid arguments of riches yielding to this qualification: That the native (*quoad Capax*, as he was born to a kingdom) should not have riches in abundance, but rather be many times necessitated for moneys and supplies; and this the rather because of Mars and Venus (who both square Jupiter the promising planet) are in partil opposition to Pars Fortuna; yet Jupiter being in reception with Mercury, who is dispositor of Pars Fortuna and Lord of the second, and the Moon being in sextile with him and the Sun, do argue a competencie of riches and the goods of fortune, although no great superfluity. And this judgement is very much fortified by the position of the Luminaries so neer very eminent fixed stars of the first magnitude.

If it be demanded whence or by what means the native's fortune or riches may come? I answer, Mercury being Lord of the second in the fourth, between the bodies of the Sun and Venus, and in reception with Jupiter; a planet in the second house prenotes them to come by the means of government, office and dignity, and shews that his fortune shall be augmented by inheritances etc., and that he shall be enriched by the antients of his family.

But, if it shall be demanded by any, whether his wealth shall continue? (for riches are often known to make themselves wings and fly away!), I answer: The Lord of the second combust, and Pars Fortuna afflicted by the malicious opposition of Mars etc. plainly portends a confiscation of estate, or at least much perplexity about it, and very great loss and damage therein. See my *Doctrine of Nativities*, cap.13. sect.3. part 1.

It is sufficiently known that this kingly native in comparison of his birth and condition was but ordinarily blessed with riches, or the goods of fortune, but many times was necessitated to borrow moneys etc. It is also fresh in the minds of many, that he was vested with the power and government of three kingdoms, namely England, Scotland and Ireland, which descended on him from his royal father King James; which is a manifest argument that his fortune came by office and government and the antients of his family. And it is also known that in process of time, by reason of a disagreement between this native and his Parliament, he was much crossed, perplexed and vexed in his estate and fortune, even at last to a confiscation thereof.

Judgements pertaining to the Third House.

The Moon being posited in the third house in Libra, the delight of Venus, denotes this native to have both brethren and sisters; and she going to a sextile of Sun and Mercury, and Venus also her dispositrix in a bi-corporeal sign, confirms the same. If we shall enquire into their condition, we shall finde them to be therein both eminent, prosperous and happy, because the Moon is in an equinoctial and cardinal sign neer the Virgin's Spike, and within the friendly rayes of Venus who disposes of her.

And if any should enquire how this native and they may accord? The answer may be, Very well. For Venus Lady of the third, casts a friendly trine to the Ascendent; and the Moon a planet upon the cusp of the third, is in an amicable aspect of the Sun, Lord of the Ascendent.

Most true it is, that this native had a brother and sisters, and their conditions were illustrious and high. And it is as true that he and they accorded wonderfully well, and were always in friendship and at peace. The like amity was between him and his kindred in general; yea, so great was his respects unto some of them that he thereby (next unto the Divine cause thereof) wrought his own overthrow.

Judgements belonging to the Fourth House.

The fierie planet Mars is Lord of the fourth house, being posited in the regal sign Sag neer the glorious beams of Venus, thence calling a benign aspect to the Ascendant; and the Sun, Lord of the Ascendant, logically in the fourth house, aptly denotes an excellent agreement between the native and his father: and this the greater because Mars, Lord of the fourth and Lord of the Ascendent, are of one nature and signification. The Moon is in sextile to the Sun also, who is the natural significator of fathers; which is another admirable argument of the unity and friendship between this native and his father; and that it should remain and continue firm and entire until one of them should be dissolved.

Considering the aforesaid arguments of agreement between the aforesaid significators, it seems improbable and most absurd and irrational to me (and I presume to all ingenious artists) that the report concerning the Duke of Buckingham's endeavouring to poyson the King, this native's father, was at all known or connived at by him. Nay, I hope (if God lend me life) to make it appear in due time to the world, that King James dyed a natural death. But it is common for the best of persons to have the basest and most unworthy reports pass on them, though never so innocent.

Judgements on the Fifth House.

This house takes cognizance of the native's issue; and we may positively conclude that the native may have children if that rule of Origanus be true – *Non dubitabis de liberis, si in 5 fuerit fortuna aliqua* – 'Thou shalt not doubt of issue, if any fortunate star or planet be posited in the fifth house'.

This native had six children by Mary, the daughter of the King of France, his Queen; namely Charls Prince of Wales, now King of Scots; James, Duke of York; Henry, Duke of Gloucester; the Lady Mary, who was espoused to the Prince of Aurange; the Lady Elizabeth, who dyed at Carisbrook in the Isle of Wight; and the Lady Henrietta, yet living.

But Mars being in the fifth house, and in square to Jupiter the Lord thereof, and afflicting Venus by his corporal presence there, doth denote much grief, trouble and unhappiness to befal the children of this native. And Jupiter being in Virgo, both in his detriment and peregrination, cleerly declares them to lead their lives in a strange land. But North Node *Caput Draconis* being posited in the fifth house, and Jupiter casting a benevolent aspect unto him there, shews they will finde honourable subsistence and moderate happiness, although nothing so auspicious and glorious as their birth might bode.

It is conspicuously true, that the children of this native have been forced to the unhappiness of seeking relief in a strange land, and there to try their fortunes, where they hitherto have been blessed with a moderate competencie, although but mean in respect of their descent.

Judgements on the Sixth House.

Both the Luminaries casting friendly aspects to the sixth house, namely the House of Sickness, and in semi-sextile to Saturn Lord thereof, denote very few diseases to afflict the native, as I noted in part in my judgements on the first house. And all the significators of sickness being free from impediment do generally portend a freedom from all perillous and violent distempers also. But as all manner of persons in the world are in one way or other subject, at some times, to some kinde of obstruction or distemper or other; so this native should according to art be subject to the gravel or stone in the kidneys or bladder, as Saturn Lord of the sixth in Scorpio, and the Moon in Libra, make known.

This native was generally very free from all manner of distempers; yet at some times he was subject to short fits of the stone, but never to his extraordinary prejudice – and this I have been credibly informed of by some persons of credit.

If any should desire to be satisfied in art concerning the fidelity or unworthiness of this native's servants unto him, I shall return a threefold answer. (1) Saturn, Lord of the sixth, is posited in Scorpio, upon the cusps of the fourth house, thence casting an opposition to the tenth, which is the house of honour and dignity – which very notably demonstrates that the servants of this native should be the meanes of the destruction of his honour and dignity by their baseness and treachery; thereby working his overthrow. (2) Mercury, the general significator of servants, is combust and in his detriment; ergo the native could hope for no good from them. And as Mercury casts a square dexter to the cusp of the second house, it may well declare that the only design of his servants should be knavishly and occultly (for Mercury is combust) to scatter and consume his estate and fortune.

This is an experienced truth; whoever hath Mercury ill posited, will never be happy in servants. (3) Although Saturn, Lord of the sixth, do oppose the tenth house, namely the dignity and honour of the native; yet he casts a sinister square quartile to the cusp of the sixth house also, which remarkably results that the ruine of this native occasioned by his servants, should perfectly prove their own precipitation.

I presume it is sufficiently known unto all that knew any thing of this native, that his servants were sufficiently and beyond measure treacherous unto him. (I speak in general only. For what is it for a person of so great a quality to have one or two, or perhaps half a score, servants honest, faithful, and loyal unto him, and all the rest perfidious?). So that he might justly have complained in the language of the Prophet Micah: 'That his chief enemies were those of his own household, and those that he most cherished and respected were the most apparent treachers to him'. As indeed, whom so fit to betray a man as he that's acquainted with his bosome secrets?

Nor is it a truth of less magnitude that this native's servants, projecting his ruine, begat their own overthrow. A man may as soon meet with a rock of diamonds upon Paul's steeple, as with an accomplished old courtier in these days. And is it not every whit as rare to see an Episcopal person? Mercury is in Sagittarius, by which may be gathered that I speak not here of ordinary servants, or those of the lower form, as of the Yeomen of the Guard, Wardrop or Wine-cellar; or of the barber, cook, baker etc. For they (poor wretches!) would willingly and with as good heart have served the Log in *Aesop*, as him whom they did, for their hire. They are those (only) of a superior degree that I speak of, who might rather have been termed his master than servants. For Saturn, who is Lord of the sixth, is very strong; and Mercury, though weak, is yet stronger than the Sun, who is *Dominus Ascendentis*.

Judgements pertaining to the Seventh House.

If we enquire into reason of this native's marriage, we shall then finde Saturn, Lord of the seventh, in the waterie sign Scorpio, posited there between the s.s. (that is, the semi-sextiles) of both the Luminaries. And Venus, the general significatrix of marriage, is in conjunction of Mars (a planet disposing of Saturn Lord of the seventh) in the fifth house; thence casting a friendly sextile *ad partem conjugii*, to the Part of Marriage, neer unto the place of that glorious star *Spica Virginis*. All which are most assured and evident testimonies of this native's propensitie to marriage.

This native did marry Henrietta Maria, the daughter of Henry the Fourth, King of France, (as was noted before, but repetition in things of this nature is very requisite, as *Cardan, seg.4. apho.85* hath well observed, *repetitie necessaria est in hac scientia etc*) in the year 1625, and consummated the same on June 23 that yeer, at Canterbury in England.

And if a reason in art were demanded concerning their agreement, whether well? The answer will be in the affirmative for the before-mentioned reasons; together with these, Venus casts a trine to the Ascendent neer the degree thereof; and the Moon from the house of Venus beholds the Sun, who is Lord of the Ascendent, with a sextile.

And that is sufficiently evidenced by the penners of this native's history, for a most eminent truth. Hear one, who of the native saith thus: 'He was a great admirer of his queen, very uxorious, seldom denying her any request, and for her sake was very civil to the old Queen of France her mother. He communicated his weightiest and most private designs unto her. Nay, there was little of moment but she was advised with concerning it.' (*Monarchy*, p.76).

Another of the same business writes thus: 'He was a most exact observer of conjugal rites, and therein for his continency much admired.'

And for the Queen's loyalty and fidelity to him we need instance in nothing else but her ardent and zealous endeavours to assist him both with supplies of men and moneys when his affairs began to grow to an ebb, in our late unhappy wars and divisions. Both being seriously considered apart, or together, it will result that their respects and observations each of and to other were reciprocal.

If any shall demand a reason why this native married a stranger? I answer, setting aside the ordinary custome of kings in such cases, the Lord of the Ascendent and seventh are of different triplicities or trigons. But that which is above all this Saturn, Lord of the seventh, was falling into the third house, and *pars conjugii* was locally there.

Judgements on the Eighth House

Let not any wonder that I treat of the kinde of the native's death in this place, and speak of his honours, dignities, friends and enemies after it; for it is only the order of the houses that leads me to it, and nothing else. To begin then.

Jupiter is Lord of the eighth house, as he governs the Fishes which descend thereon, and he is in Virgo in his detriment. But Mars being Lord of the fourth, and having triplicity in the eighth and in quartile to Jupiter also, may be admitted anareta, that is, the interficient or killing planet. The Lord of the Ascendent is in Sagittarius with *Cor Scorpii*, a violent fixed star of the first magnitude, which is one testimony of a violent death. The Lord of the eighth squared by Mars, and the eighth house also, from a violent sign, is another argument of a violent death. *Cor Leonis*, or the heart of the Lyon in the Ascendent, and *Caput Algol* in the tenth house; Venus, Lady of the tenth, in conjunction with Mars, in square of Jupiter, and Saturn casting an opposition to the tenth from fixed signs, are most assured arguments of a violent death.

Divers astrologers have been otherwise perswaded, having seen his nativity, but upon very slender grounds in my opinion; and now they are convinced by the event. For a violent death he did die, namely by having his head severed from his body, and this before the Banquetting House at White-Hall, on January 30, 1648.

But more of this in its proper place.

Judgements pertinent to the Ninth House.

We finde upon the cusp of the ninth, Aries, a movable sign, and the Moon on the cusp of the third in a moveable sign also, namely Libra; which plainly portends a desire or propensity in the native to travel, or to go some long voyage or journey. But the Moon being in opposition to the ninth from cardinal signs, argues very much infelicity unto the native therein.

If it be demanded, which way should he travel or voyage? I answer, Eastward, or South-East; for Aries is upon the cusp of the ninth, and the Lords of the Ascendent and the ninth are in Sagittarius a South-East sign.

Most true it is that this native was not only propense or desirous to travel, but did travel into Spain. It was thought (by some) for the love of the Infanta of Spain, by others, for honour and pleasure. But be it for what it will, travel he did, but gained neither honour nor the Infanta by his voyage; but on the contrary was subject to misfortune therein.

And indeed, so unprosperous was the time he set forward on, namely February 17, 1623, (as these several evidences make appear), that he could not have elected a worse.

1. Mars upon the radical place of Sun.
2. Moon in the sixth of the radix.
3. Venus in square to Sun's radical place.

4. Sun in square to his own place.
5. Mercury in square to the places of Mars and Venus, and in opposition to the place of Jupiter.
6. Moon in the revolution in square to Saturn one being in opposition, the other in square to the tenth of the radix.

I spare to speak at large of this strange deliverance from captivity, being in the French court disguised, in the way of his returning home with the Duke of Buckingham. Ergo, from the testimonies of his travel, I come to those of his religion.

And truly, according to natural causes, he should have been a great honourer if not an adorer of religion, and of the clergie also; for the Lord of the ninth in the figure is posited in Sagittarius, the joy and delight of Jupiter, and there in conjunction of Venus, casting an amicable aspect to the Ascendent. But Jupiter his dispositor being in his detriment and in [square] to him, and the Sun also, did bode no good in the end to this native from the clergie; nor indeed from them to him, but rather that they should be prejudicial the one to the other.

It is very certain that he was a great friend unto religion and a great adorer thereof in his lifetime, and at his death discovered himself to be the same by his pious speech on the scaffold, in which he had these words: 'Sirs! My conscience in religion I think is very well known to all the world, and therefore I declare before you all, that I die a Christian according to the profession of the Church of England,' etc.

And for his great affection and zeal to the clergie, hear what one of his observators says: 'He was a great lover (if not too much) of the clergie, and highly advanced them… And that his indulgence unto them did in part procure unto himself the people's hate.' And when I seriously consider the detriment of Jupiter and the square that is between the Sun and he, I am much inclinable to believe that his cockering of the clergie, and their ambitious (if not presumptuous) use of his favours and indulgences, was the very first visible step to his overthrow and ruine. But he with his kingdom did not only fall; the bishops and Church accompanied them.

Nativity of the Late King Charles

Judgements belonging to the Tenth House.

The angles of the figure fixed, and Venus governess of the tenth in an amicable aspect of the Ascendent, are arguments of much honour, dignity and renown to happen to the native. And *Orig. de effectib. fol.699.* saith, the Sun *in 4 gloriam perpetuam presertim cum regia stella denotat*. And it is very true, the Sun is with the Scorpion's Heart, which is a kingly fixed star. And it is a very great testimony of the native's honour and dignity, and denotes him to be high in his renown.

But now, if we enquire whether the native's honour and glory shall be durable or continue to the end? I answer negatively, they cannot. For Mars is in conjunction of Venus, Lady of the tenth, in a fiery sign, neer violent fixed stars; and Saturn (an enemy to the honours and ornaments of nature, as well as nature itself) is in direct opposition to the cusp of the tenth; which plainly intimates a subversion of the native's dignities, honour and eminency. And this the more certain and (when it comes) violent, because the afflicters of the native's greatness are the two superiour planets, and both of them malefiques.

I shall not need to insert here the sad misfortune that befell this princely native, because I shall meet with a most convenient place for that anon. Besides (if I should not) the world hath heard of it on both ears already, and that super-sufficiently.

If any shall demand – how it should happen that this native should reign in honour and glory so long as he did, seeing the significators of dignity afflicted? I answer: Although Venus, Lady of the tenth, be afflicted by the corporal presence of Mars, yet she casts a trine to the Ascendent; and Jupiter, a significator of soveraignty, casts a benign ray to the tenth house. But Jupiter being, as I told you before, both weak and in detriment and peregrination, and in square of Mars likewise, did cleerly argue that the time he did reign, his soveraignty and renown were with much difficulty and trouble kept up and preserved. And indeed, those eminent fixed stars in the chief angles of his nativity, were certain arguments of his attaining to an excellent degree of honour and dignity; but the planets not concurring, were the occasion of its discontinuance – according to that known aphorism of Ptolomy, *Cent.29*:

Stella fixae in angulis, admirabiles felicitates adserunt, quas tamen plerumque calamitatibus insigniunt, nisi et Planetae ad foelicitatem conveniant.

And indeed his honour and preferment did end or determine in an unusual calamity, as in the history of his life before-mentioned may more largely appear.

This therefore shall serve in this place, for an account astrological of the native's honour, dignity and power.

Judgements on the Eleventh House.

No sooner do I cast mine eyes on the eleventh house of this nativity, but a testimony of treachery plainly presents itself, namely *Cauda Draconis* in the flegmatique sign Cancer, intercepted there; which is an undeniable and never failing testimony of the treachery and infidelity of friends; and of many contentions, strifes and quarrels between the native and them. Yea, when he hath the greatest hopes, they shall then prove the greatest back-sliders in friendship to him.

I could instance in the genitures of divers persons of eminencie who have notably experienced the perfidiousness of friends, by having *Cauda*, the South Node, in their eleventh house. As Gustavus Adolphus, that victorious and warlike King of Sweden, and those two renowned emperours, Ferdinand and Charls the Fifth. And that great and most eminently learned Divine, Philip Melanchthon, with divers others. And it is most certain that if the South Node, the Tayl, posited in the ninth doth destroy the religion and moral honesty of the native; and if in the tenth, his dignities and honour: so by its position in the eleventh house it makes shipwrack of his hopes, and absolutely separates betwixt him and his friends.

But besides this we have other testimonies of this native's poor assistance from friends; namely Mars and Venus both opposing the cusp of the eleventh, and Jupiter sending a square thereunto; which pertinently proves that his friends, and hopes of them, will prescind and vanish from him in his greatest extremity, and when he hath most need of their assistance.

Lastly, I observe Mercury, Lord of the eleventh, to be in opposition thereunto; and he combust and in detriment, in square of his dispositor and separating from the Lord of the Ascendent; of which position hear *Origanus, fol.706. Si dominus 11:*

Separatus fuerit a domino Ascendentis, natus paucos habebit amicos, et abhorrebunt eum ejus socii et amici ipseque cos. Haly *de judic. Astrorum, pars 5.c.13.* saith the same.

Now, for a verification of these astrological axioms (for they are such) let it be remembered that this illustrious person (whose nativity we handle) in his greatest and most to be lamented wants and extremities, and when he had most need of, and occasion for, to make use of the assistance of friends, they then most of all deserted him and turned their backs upon his wants and necessities. And this is conspicuously seen, as a vein particular by itself cleerly running along the whole history of his life; I therefore need not descend unto particulars. And thus much concerning this native's friends.

Judgements proper to the Twelfth House.

By the judgements of the last house we finde the native blessed but with few friends, it will therefore roundly follow, that by how much the fewer his friends are, by so much the more numerous will be his enemies; the condition, danger, and power of whom, is to be enquired from this house.

The Lord of the twelfth and Ascendent in conjunction with Mercury in a double-bodyed sign, portends many dangerous enemies unto the native; and the Lord of the seventh in a fixed sign, on the cusp of the fourth, the same. And as the Lord of the seventh is stronger by far than the Lord of the Ascendent, we may rationally conclude that the adversaries of the native will be found too powerful for him, and therefore be the more likely to prevail against him. And if I may presume to give a natural reason for this native's suffering, imprisonment and captivity, he being (then) a King, and chief Governour of three nations; I shall answer in the words of that worthy author, D. Origanus – 'Infortunes in angles are the certain occasioners of restraint or captivity'. And he telleth us moreover – 'That the same position was the cause of Henry Cornelius Agrippa's imprisonment'. But some may object that both the Infortunes here are not in angles. I answer, it is true; we cannot say that both the infortunes are in angles because Mars is in Sagittarius in the fifth house. But Saturn, his being in the fourth in a fixed sign so diametrically opposing the tenth house, and he Lord of the seventh, is every whit as malevolent a position, as if both had been posited in angles.

But Johannes Hispalenses (as quoted by Origanus) is more plain – *Dominus duodecima si fuerit junctos domino Ascendentis, et fuerint ambo in domo 4. et fuerit dominus Ascendentis infortunatus, natus in carcerem conjicietur*, fol.715.

In English thus:

'If the Lord of the twelfth shall be in corporal conjunction with the Lord of the Ascendent, and both of them happen to be in the fourth house; and if there the Lord of the Ascendent happen to be unfortunate, the person that is then born shall be hurled or cast into prison, or overtaken with captivity'. One planet is Lord both of the twelfth and Ascendent in this nativity and he is posited in the fourth house most unfortunate, the very weakest planet in the whole figure, and may therefore well signifie restraint or bondage to the native.

But now if we may enquire into the kinde and condition of this native's enemies at large, we shall finde them to be persons of an indifferent condition, and of the most inferiour degree; (but joyned strength proves the strongest) according to that ancient rule of Haly, *De judic. Astror. pars 5. cap.14. fol.237* – *Si quando dominus domus inimicorum fuerit in angulo vel succedenti, habens ibi aliquam dignitatem, inimici nati erunt nobiles et potentes: Sed si fuerit cadens ab angulo aut peregrinus, vel sub radiis solis, aut in suo casu, erunt debiles et in malo statu*. Which in effect tells us this in plain English – That if the Lord of the twelfth shall be posited in an angle (as here he is) or succedent house, having any dignity there (here he is the weakest in the scheam), the enemies of the native shall be persons of honour and eminencie, etc. But if he shall be peregrine (as he is here) or cadent, or under the Sun's beams, or in his fall, the enemies of the native shall then be rustical, unlearned, weak, and (in respect of their quality) not much to be considered or taken notice of.

I need not take notice of the kinde or manner of this native's imprisonment or captivity, nor of the kindes or degrees of men that were his most professed enemies; for the one, and the other, is sufficiently known. I will therefore conclude with this memento, that he was captivated, and thereby suffered restraint and imprisonment; and for the degrees or kindes of his enemies at large, they seem wondrous well to be depainted by the later part of the aphorism lately cited.

Nativity of the Late King Charles

Thus I have finished my general judgments of the twelve houses of this nativity, and therein given you a general astrological character both plain and true (but not drawn absolutely to the life, as it might have been) of the life and fortune of this most unhappy and unfortunate Prince. But for a more particular account of the same, I shall request the reader's patience to attend what follows.

AN
ASTROLOGICAL ACCOUNT,
Of the last eleven Yeers of this
NATIVE'S LIFE.
Being a brief Compendium of the most eminent Actions that hapned in
GREAT BRITAINE
within the compass of that time.

Because the most important actions of this native's life brake forth in the yeer 1639, being the 39th yeer of his age, (notwithstanding the plot of his ruine – and indeed the destruction of these three nations – was laid long before, as appears at large by the discovery thereof, in Mr. Sanderson's *History*, fol.287). I shall there begin my particular judgements of the fortune of this (once) most mighty Prince, and continue it to his death; and as neer as I am able (within the limits of these particular yeers, namely, eleven), give you an account of the most material actions he then underwent, and their peculiar reasons in art, be they either of good or bad consequence.

Before I come to speak of this revolution it will not be amiss to acquaint you that in the beginning of the yeer, namely March 27, this native went in person towards Scotland to appease the mutinous (or rather rebellious) covenanters; which multitude he for a time reduced to a seeming quietness. But alas! he going about so eminent an action in so unfortunate a time, gave those his adversaries an advantage by their then pretended retreat, to prejudice him at the last with the greater violence.

At the time he undertook this matter, the cruel planet Saturn was then in opposition to the Ascendent of his radix, and in square to the Midheaven and fourth house; Mars then neer *Caput Medusa* in the tenth, thence casting a malignant square to the Ascendent also. And in *Figura mundi*, *Cauda*, the South Node, was culminating, and Saturn and Mars in square from fixed signs; and Jupiter in square of Mercury.

All which testimonies, according to the canons of Astrologie, presignified nothing but treachery and very hard fortune to the native (then) in his designs both publike and private; loss of his honour and reputation; many scandals and disgraces from his enemies; himself subject to many great streights and inconveniencies.

To be brief, he patched up a peace with the Scots, which was observed but slenderly on their parts. Yea, so slenderly, that in their squirting papers presently after, they fastned (or endeavoured so to do) most notorious scandals, not onely upon the native, but the whole English nation which he governed. And together with their scurilities, they mixed threats of another invasion, which in August 1640 the English nation permitted them to perform.

Malum principium, malus finis sequitur.
'All ill beginnings, such conclusions have'.

And so I am properly led to the revolution of this yeer.

Judicium Astrologicum.

In the figure [overleaf] we have the regal sign Sagittarius ascending on the Eastern finitor, the degree thereof being the radical place of Venus, and the Governess of the tenth house, both here and in the radix; and posited in the Ascendent retrograde. There, in conjunction of Jupiter, which position seems to portend the beginning of this revolution to be honourable and auspicious to the native; according to that aphorism of Schonerus – *Dominus* M.C. *in ascendente revolutionis, signif.* etc. The Lord of the Midheaven in the Ascendent of a revolution prenotes both honour and happiness to the native. And most true it is, the yeer did begin with smiles; for this kingly native then newly was returned triumphantly home, from reducing the Scots to obedience; the City of London nobly entreat him, and there are great preparations for a Parliament. All things seemed to sound well; no jar at all in the musique.

And this his happiness and felicity is considerably augmented unto by the birth of a son, namely Henry Duke of Gloucester, on July 8 day,

Nativity of the Late King Charles

Revolutio Solis ad punctum Radicis
November 19, 1639. 32 hours 14 minutes P.M.

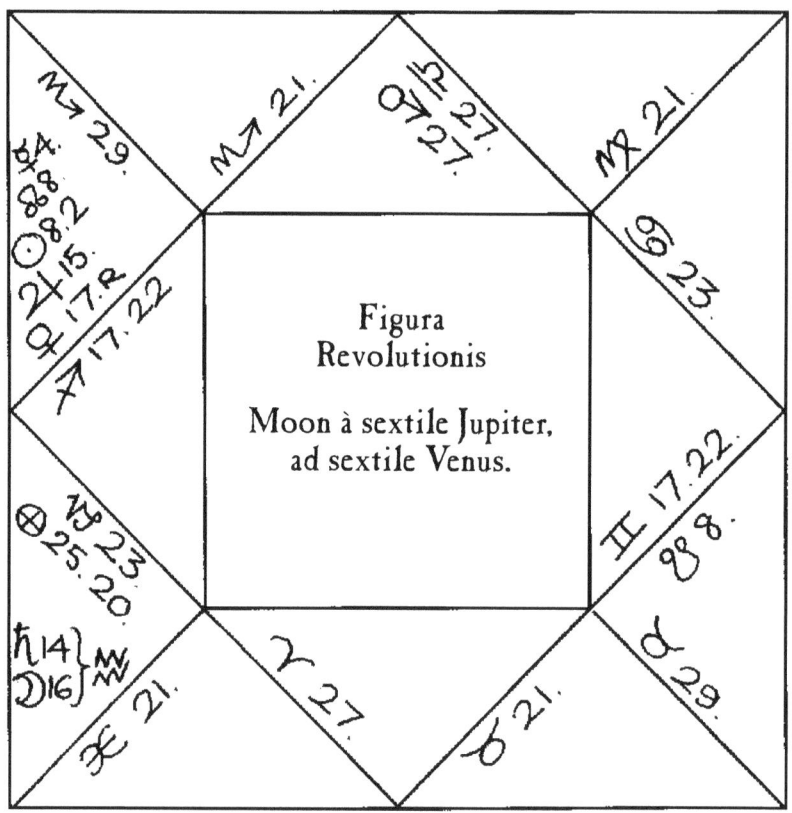

as is very notably seen by the revolution where Venus, Lady of the fifth, is in conjunction with Jupiter, Lord of the fifth in the radix, and posited in the Ascendent.

But what avails an hour's sunshine in the morning when it is but the forerunner of a showrie day? For we finde Mars here posited upon the very cusp of the house of honour and dignity, being in detriment and in quartile to *pars fortunae*, the Part of Fortune, in the second. Which is a plain argument that the honour and eminency of this native will be in danger of being undermined, and that by a sort of persons which should seem to be his most pretended friends, for Mars is Lord of the eleventh house. But this is not all, for the estate of this native is in much jeopardy, and in danger of damage and prejudice. For (besides Mars,

Nativity of the Late King Charles

his affliction of *pars fortunae*), we finde Saturn in the second house in corporal conjunction of Luna.

Infortunae in secunda revolutionis, significat quod natus multa dispendia faciet secundum naturam infortunae, saith Schoner, fol.198. 'The position of an Infortunate planet in the second house of a revolution denotes much loss and expence to the native in his estate, by men and things of the nature of the Infortune which shall be found there'.

Now if we consider how notoriously this native was bespattered before his calling a Parliament, and his being intrencht on by the Scots and perswaded by his Councel to curry favour with them etc. It is testimony enough of his dishonour, and of the disrespect he received. And then his going against the Scots was so costly to him, that his treasure was so far wasted, that the Parliament when they sate, namely April 13, were enforced to borrow some thousands of pounds of the City. But such was this native's misfortune that his greatest actions in the last three parts of the yeer were commenced at most unhappy times, and *rarus principii est exitus bonni mali*.

As to instance in same: (1). April 13 he assembled the Parliament. The Moon then was with the South Node neer *Caput Medusae* in square of Saturn, and Mars in square to the tenth of the revolution; Mercury in quartile to the Ascendent of the radix, and Venus squares her radical place; which were plain testimonies that so great an assembly so convening could not continue long together. Neither did they, for May 5 following, they were dissolved.

(2). On October the 26 he ratified and confirmed peace with the Scots. Venus then Lady of the tenth of the revolution was in square of Saturn, Lord of the seventh in the radix, from fixed signs. Ergo, no good time to conclude with an enemy.

(3). November 3. The Long Parliament began to sit. The Sun and the Moon were then in Scorpio in conjunction of Mercury, Lord of the seventh in the revolution, and upon the cusp of the twelfth in that figure, in square to the Ascendent and seventh of the radix; and all of them in quartile to Saturn, Lord of the seventh of the radix. Most of the planets being fixed was one main reason (perhaps) of that Parliament's continuing so long a time, and of the native's ruine by them.

It is also worthy consideration; Saturn being in Aquarius, and stronger by far than either the Sun or the Moon, or Jupiter who was Lord of the

Nativity of the Late King Charles

tenth house, in the figure of the Parliament's first sitting. But I shall refer that to the more able students in this art, for it is only fit to feed their understandings. And so I conclude my Judgements of this yeer's actions.

Revolutio Solis ad punctum Radicis,
November 19th, 2 hours 41minutes P.M. 1640

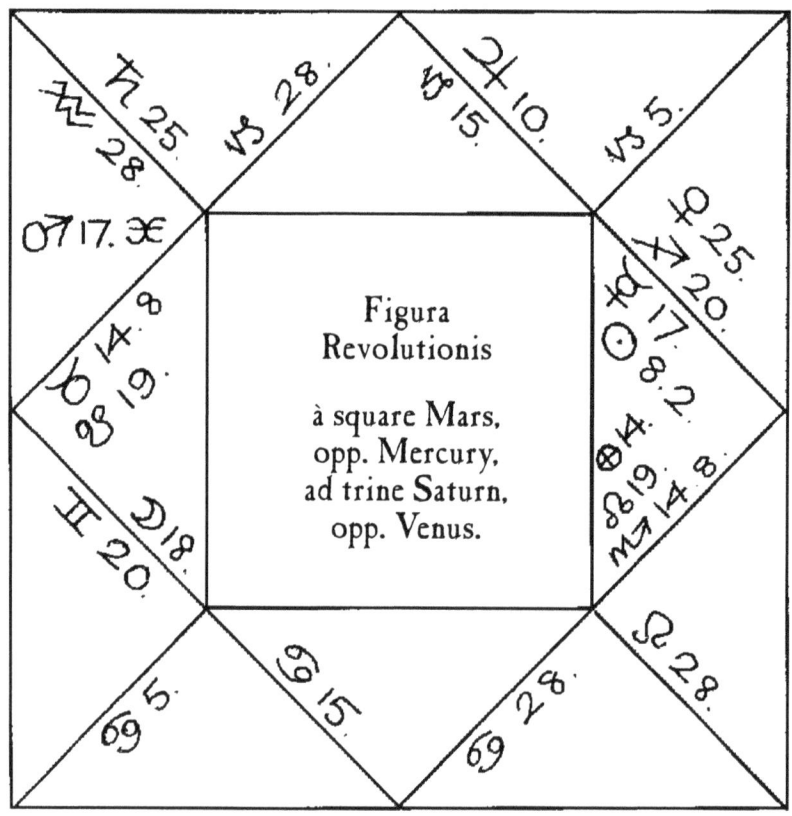

Fortuna ad T. Saturn by direction.

Judicium Astrologicum.

In this yeer's revolution we find the South Node in the Ascendent, and the figure itself directly opposite to the figure of the world this year, which is an ill position and might therefore very well bode unto the native many crosses and troubles, and much ado to keep up his former honor and repute in the minds of men. Many ignominies and disgraces should be heaped upon him, even with much violence. Indeed it is more than probable that the native should this yeer be surrounded with a sea of sorrows and vexations, for Venus, Lady of the Ascendent, is posited in the eighth in square to Mars in the twelfth. *Cauda draconis in ascendente revolutionis, significat Melancholiam* etc. The position of the Dragon's Tayl in the Ascendent of a revolution prenotes the native to be troubled with melancholy, and much trouble and grief of minde. And this is augmented by the Moon's being in square to Mars, Lord of the seventh, and her opposition to Venus, Lady of the yeer.

When the Lord of the Ascendent or the Moon shall be in square or opposition of the Infortunes, the native in that year shall suffer much loss and detriment, saith J. Schoner. And here you see the aphorism in both parts of it fully take place, and must therefore have its fuller signification. And as Mars the afflicting planet is Lord of the seventh, and in the twelfth, it portends that the native's publique and private enemies will plot and contrive things very maliciously and treacherously against him; and this most probably under the masque of religion, for Mars is in sextile of Jupiter and in reception with him also. The Part of Fortune to the terms of Saturn by direction prejudices the native in his estate.

To verify these aphorisms and predictions we shall finde that this native was this yeer much abused by scandalous and scurrilous libels and reports; he is thought strangely of by the Parliament concerning Ship-money, and some patents etc. He is much perplexed and troubled about some pretended new discoveries, by reason of which Lord Finch with others is forced to flie, whose flight fastned many obloquies and reproaches on the native, which help much to encrease his grief and trouble of minde.

The Earl of Strafford and Bishop of Canterbury are questioned; the King pleads for bishops, is over-ruled therein, and episcopacy turned out of doors by the force and multitudes of the Presbyterians in their petitions from all parts of the nation. Earl of Strafford is condemned; the King desires to save him, but cannot; he is grieved very much thereat. Let his demands be what they will, he is still over-ruled; a necessity thereof is pretended as affairs then flood. Pretended plots of the Papists discovered; this native is thought a great friend of theirs, and is ill thought of therefore by many. Many giddy-headed people in multitudes press to Westminster and Lambeth crying for justice.

These very things, with divers others, most cleerly demonstrate the truth of the aforesaid predictions, even to admiration! and are indeed part of the malicious effects signified by the position of the Sun and the Moon in Scorpio in square to his Ascendent at the time of the Parliament's first sitting, November 3, and their square to Saturn Lord of the seventh house.

In the next place we come to consider the condition of the native's estate; and that should not be very glorious or splendid for Mercury, Lord of the second house, is combust, and in opposition to the Moon in the second; and both of them in square to Mars. And (as I told you before) the Part of Fortune is now directed to the terms of Saturn. All which signifies loss or want of substance, and much unnecessary and vain expence of treasure. And Saturn casting a malicious square to the Part of Fortune confirms it. I might also take notice of the Part of Fortune being posited in the seventh house, which hath no better signification than any of the arguments before mentioned; if we consider what a design this yeer was contrived concerning the militia. Besides, this yeer the native married a daughter (namely the Lady Mary) to the Prince of Aurange; the Scots also cry out for moneys and bring in their large accounts, and the King in ordinary matters is much necessitated.

But notwithstanding the great grief and trouble this native underwent in some things, yet in others again he had honour, pleasure, and delight; although nothing in comparison of the other. For Jupiter is upon the cusp of the tenth house in trine to the Ascendent; which was a very significant testimony of honour etc. And indeed, both Lords and Commons, and City, did in some measure indulge him, and made some modest and honourable addresses unto him; what they were, you may finde in the History of his Life. But Mars being in square of the Sun, soon clip't the wings of this good signification, that it lasted not long. But Mars being in reception with Jupiter, and in sextile of him also, presaged the lesser prejudice at present, although it be more than probable it was the foundation of some further evil.

Nor was it less than a high and transcendent honour, for this princely native to marry his daughter to a neighbour prince; which accident seems admirably well to be signified by Jupiter's being Lord of the fifth in the radix, and here posited upon the cusp of honour and dignity; thence casting a trine to the Ascendent; and Venus in the revolution upon the cusp of the fifth in the radix, disposed of by Jupiter. All which are eminent testimonies of this native's honour and of the pleasure and delight he should have had in his children.

But, before I conclude, let it be remembered that this native passed the Bill for Triennial Parliaments, and the Bill of Attainder against the Earl of Strafford, this year on May the tenth; at which time the Moon was in her radical place in square of Mars, and Saturn Lord of the seventh of the radix in square of the Sun Lord of the Ascendent. Two transits of as mischievous a tendency as may be. The Irish Rebellion brake forth immediately after. Thus much for this yeer's actions.

Revolutio Solis ad punctum Radicis,
November 19, 8 hours 29 minutes P.M. 1641.

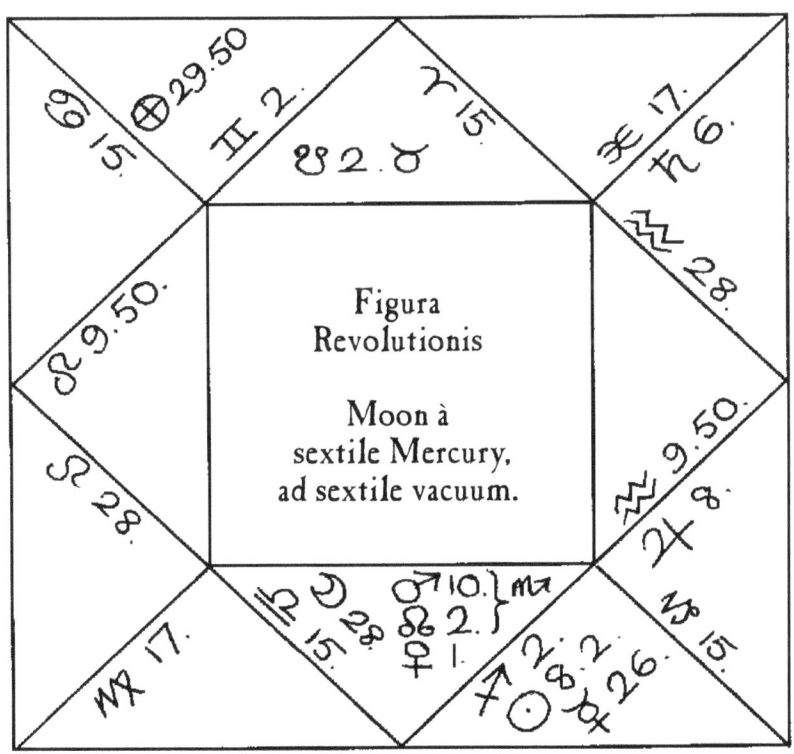

Judicium Astrologicum.

The directions beginning to operate this yeer 1641 are –
1. M.C. ad square to Jupiter.
2. Asc. ad square to Venus.

This yeer's actions favour much of the last yeer's infelicitie, for here we have *Cauda Draconis* in the tenth house, neer the degree that culminates in the radix. As if there were some design or conspiracy contriving against the native's honour and estimation. And this principally from those of the vulgar sort, or the meer rabble-rout, for Taurus is an earthy sign. But Saturn being in square to the Sun, Lord of the Ascendent both here and in the radix, and in the dignities of Jupiter, presages prejudice to this native, from or by reason of a more eminent sort of persons who work underground, privately and secretly, and in a clandestine manner carry on their designs to the great prejudice of this native, and to the almost abrogating of his hopes, as Saturn in the eighth house is square to the eleventh, aptly signifies. And that which is worst of all, these ill portents will not prove like a flash of lightning or the brisking of the wine in the glass, and be as soon gone as seen; but on the contrary will be carried on zealously, and with great affection and secrecie, and therefore may bode a greater and more considerable mischief to the native, for Mars Lord of the tenth, is in square to Jupiter the dispositor of Saturn from fixed signes; which argues the tedious continuance and duration of these evils. And Mars here upon the radical place of Saturn, in opposition to the tenth house, makes them the more violent and cruel.

These predictions are notably well verified by the plots, the conspiracies and secret connivances, that were set on foot in Scotland, immediately after this kingly native's return thence. Insurrections and tumults here at home threatning both King and bishops. The insolencies and arrogancies of the vulgar, rising with clubs and staves against they knew not what. The unhappy breach between the King and Parliament on January 3 concerning the Five Members; an action most unhappy! hapning at so malicious and unfortunate a time, namely upon a square of Saturn and Mars. And Mars then upon the radical place of Sun; the Moon also in opposition of Mercury and Venus; the King leaves London upon the tenth of the same month, came no more at it, until he was brought thither to receive his tryal, sentence, and death.

Nativity of the Late King Charles

It was a yeer that in most matters carryed misfortune in the very face of it; for after he had left London, he travels with a perplexed minde northward, and in April came before Hull, and on the twenty-third demanded entrance therein but was denyed by Sir John Hotham. The Moon the same day was neer the South Node in the radix and Mars upon the opposite place of his Ascendent, and in square to the tenth, and the Sun upon the opposite place of Mars in the revolution.

Immediately after this, the Parliament raise an army, appoint the Earl of Essex their General, and on August 22 the King set up his standard at Nottingham. The Moon then in square to the Sun and Jupiter. The Sun being in direct square to his own place, neer the oppositions of Jupiter and Saturn, Jupiter being Lord of the tenth in the figure. But his coming to a trine of Mars first, who is Lord of the tenth in the revolution, did favour his designs a little at the first, and was perhaps (next unto our sins) one main reason why our Civil and most unnatural War remained so long. Observe the figure thereof:

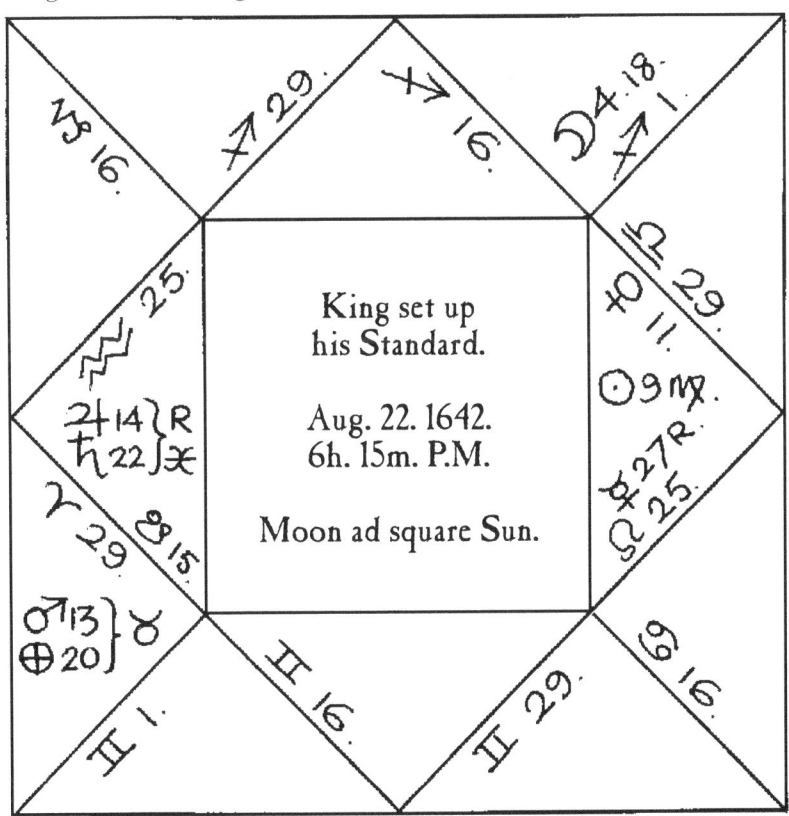

Nativity of the Late King Charles

To add to what was said before, this figure is directly opposite to that of the radix. But to go on, we are now preparing for battels apace, all things are in readiness, both armies ordered and disciplined accordingly. And at Edg-hill in Warwickshire on October 23 they meet and engage. The conflict was sharp, and many men fell on both sides; at which day's actions I think no true-born Englishman had, or hath reason to rejoyce, notwithstanding the great division or rather confusion then among us.

Shortly after this, the King advancing toward London, was opposed by the Earl of Essex his army at Brainford, on November the 12th and 13th days. Mars being then retrograde and in detriment, and upon the M.C. of the radix, and neer the place of the South Node in the revolution in opposition to the place of Venus, who was Governess of the tenth and fourth houses. Which might aptly portend the worst to happen to this native in that engagement or undertaking.

Now as we have observed the arguments of infortunacie in this yeer's revolution, it is requisite that we take a survey of those testimonies of good that there are, although they be far the lesser in number. And (1) we finde the Sun, Lord of the Ascendent, in trine unto it. (2) The Moon in partil sextile to the second house, and trine to the Part of Fortune, and in sextile to Mercury, Lord of the eleventh and third houses. Which argue the native active and industrious and very zealous in promoting his designs; and promised him some (such thing as) alliance from some of his friends and allies; but Mercury, Lord of the eleventh, in opposition to the Part of Fortune, shewed a sting to come along with the honey of friendship, which questionless had he avoyded, he had taken the better part.

The affairs of this native were promoted notably by him, rather violently or torrent-like, and he was active in person with his armies, and took divers places as Shepton Mallet, Banbury; he garrison'd Oxford etc. But for the assistance he received from the gentry of those countreys he came in, some of his own party help to scatter and consume it, as Mercury's opposition to the Part of Fortune well denotes.

It is notoriously known that this native had now, or neer this time, the service of the two Princes Maurice and Rupert, his nephews, namely sons to the Queen of Bohemia, his sister. Mercury is Lord of the third in the revolutional figure, and so affected as before. Querie – Whether the assistance or service of these two Princes did not rather hinder than

Nativity of the Late King Charles

help him? I have seen the nativities of those princes, and one of them, namely Rupert, his Ascendent is in square to the place of the Sun in this radix. And the Sun in his genesis in partil square to the Moon's place in this radix, which by Apho.33 of *Ptol. Centil.* prenotes this native to have but poor assistance from or by reason of the services of this Prince. I spare to speak here of the underhand actions (by some, termed treacheries) this Prince was supposedly guilty of, and at some times questioned for, since divers others have plainly done it already. But this may demonstratively prove – It had been far better for this native to have been without him, and his greatest services.

The geniture of Prince Maurice is nothing so malicious and contrary to this native's; nor do they exactly agree that he should have been thought a fit assistant in any personal service of this native's, for both his Moon and Mars are neer the place of Saturn in this illustrious nativity.

But if we shall take notice of another cause (as great) of this native's (this yeer's) misfortune, as was the revolution, we shall finde it to be the two directions mentioned before, namely M.C. *ad* square to Jupiter, Asc. *ad* square to Venus. The former of which, Origamus tells us, hath these significations – M.C. *ad [square Jupiter] nato causa legum, judiciorum, sententiarumque, multa gravamina significantur. Habebit judices et jurisconsultos parum aquos, qui ex invidia nato obesse, eumque dignitatibus et officiis exuere studebunt, sed ex parie frustra. Sentiet etiam a spiritualibus molestias, corumque causa de sua substantia aliquid amittere cogetur.*

Nor hath the Asc. *ad* square Venus, much better significations. I need not trouble you with the English of these words, for they are aptly Englished in the aforesaid discourse, and will receive more significant explanation the next yeer; for then the effects thereof will be in force. But if any desire to read the English thereof they may repair to *fol.189. part 1.* of *The Doctrine of Nativities* lately published. And so I end my Observations on this yeer's actions.

Nativity of the Late King Charles

Revolutio Solis as punctum Radicis,
November 19, 1642. 14 hours 17minutes P.M.

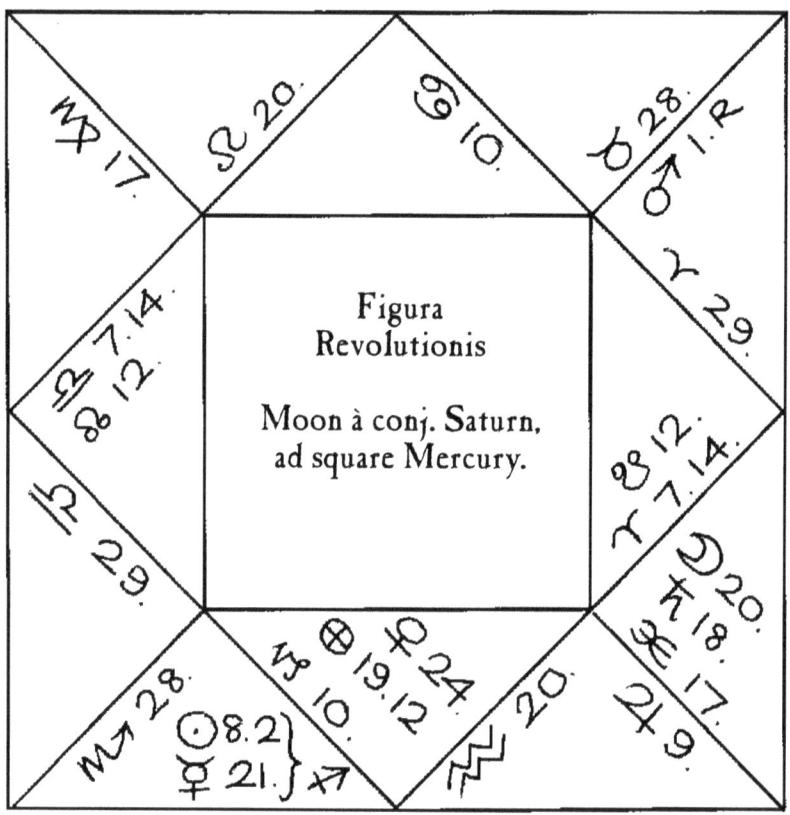

As the direction of the M.C. to the square of Jupiter rendered this native unsuccessful and unfortunate in his counsels and state affairs, and things of more public concernment, so the Ascendent to the square of Venus crosses him in matters and businesses more private, or relating to his particular domestical affairs; as loss or want of moneys, much of his estate strangely consumed etc. Many discontents of ill consequence to happen between this native and his Queen, occasioned by the distrusts and jealousies of Mercurial men or women; and perhaps through a want or necessity of moneys – for the direction happens in the second house, and in the dignities of Mercury. It shews also many discontents and disgraces to the Queen and divers troubles to attend her; and this judgement is

Nativity of the Late King Charles

unhappily seconded by the existence of *Cauda* in the seventh of the revolution.

It is most true that this native did suffer prejudice, not onely in his publike but private affairs, and principally for want of treasure; and that that he had was wasted and consumed. Yea, so great were his necessities that (I am credibly informed) an eminent Officer of this native's, wanting pay, made bold to sell part of the wood that was ordained for the Court's use, at Oxford. And it is as true that some kinde of discontent happened between this native and his Queen, which was made known by the letters that were intercepted (afterward) at Knaseby; for in some of them, bearing date this yeer, she charged dissembling upon him. Whence might easily be gathered, there was some private discontent then happened between them, the cause of which their prudence might prevent the world from taking knowledge of. And for the publique disparagement and disgrace that should have hapned to the Queen this year according to the former predictions, what could be more significant and plain, than her being voted and proclaimed a traytor to the Government of that nation of which her husband was King?

But now if we consider the revolution seriously, we shall finde Mercury in the radical place of Venus, and the North Node in the Ascendent, which declare health of body and (in general) peace of minde to this native. He is addicted to many delights and sportive recreations and may have divers addresses made unto him, and be courted and complemented by many; and that by persons of eminent quality, for the Moon is in sextile to Venus, Lady of the Ascendent. But she being in conjunction of Saturn in the sixth house seems to darken the beauty and excellencie of those benign presages – which suspition is augmented by the Sun, who is Lord of the Ascendent of the radix, his being in square of Jupiter and both of them subterranean in the house of Jupiter, which portends some unhappy prejudice or misfortune to befal the native by the means or designs of clergie-men and lawyers, (for under the signification of Jupiter such persons are placed).

The native was the most part of this yeer blessed with health of body and pleasure of minde; divers addresses were made unto him. The Universitie of Oxford sacrifice both moneys and plate to his use, so do the gentry of the countrey, seeing his affairs going backward for want of money. He is courted by divers, and in particular by the Embassadour

Extraordinary from France. But is maligned and much prejudiced by clergie-men and lawyers, for the then Parliament, who were most of them of the Long Robe, were very active to the detriment of this native's proceedings. And about the same time the Presbyterians in their pulpits piped many thousands out of the City of London and the associated countreys, to help the Lord (as they then whined it, though afterward they turned their tale) against the Mighty.

But to go on: we finde the South Node in the seventh house, namely the house of publique enemies; and the Lord of the seventh in his detriment, which is plaine argument that the native's adversaries or publick enemies should be surrounded with fear and danger and subject to many misfortunes and losses. And Venus, Lady of the Ascendent, is locally in the fourth house in conjunction with *Pars Fortuna*, promising success to the native in lands, houses, strongholds, fortifications, and the like; but by Mars his square to her there, there should be much opposition threatned to the native in such actions, and many strifes, and strong bickerings between the native and his enemies. But Venus being more potent than Mars, it is easie to say and determine which of the two will overcome.

It is very true that this native was fortunate in taking of towns and castles etc. As Marlborough, Liscard, Saltash, Cyrencester, Bremingham, Liechfield, Burton-upon-Trent, Bristol, Dorchester, Portland, Exceter, Dartmouth etc., which also proves his prevalency against his enemies; for armies in contest are like to the weights of a clock, as the one goes up the other proportionably goes down. But as Venus was squared by Mars, Lord of the seventh, so he received some prejudice and infortunacy also (though not so great as was his success) by the power and force of his enemies. As to instance in the surrender of Reading, Taunton and Bridgwater, and the being forced off from Glocester siege, with the loss at Newbery's first fight etc. Besides, so great was the Parliament's prejudice now to the King, and so ill they resented his actions, that they order a new Broad Seal.

Let the modest and ingenuous reader take notice that I mention these things, not as if I rejoyced at the victory of the one, or vanquishing of the other, but as they relate to my task in hand, and with sorrow, that so much English blood and treasure was consumed and exhausted to the almost irreparable damage and prejudice, both of the (then) King and

Nativity of the Late King Charles

Kingdom. Nothing more being considerable in the actions of this yeer, I here conclude its Judgements.

Revolutio Solis ad punctum Radicis,
November 19th, 20 hours 5 minutes P.M. 1643.

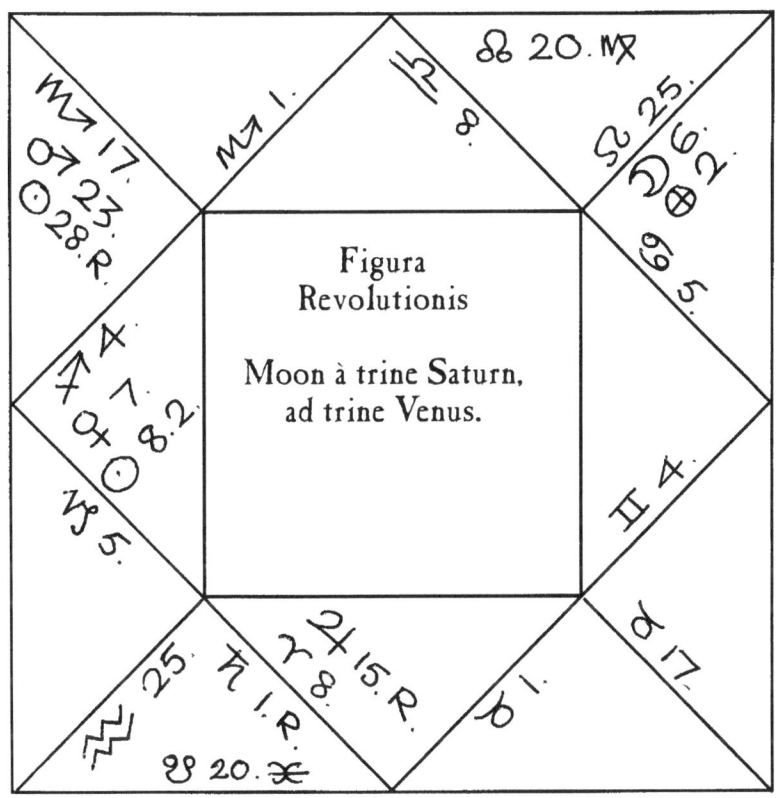

M.C. ad T. Saturn per direct.

Judicium Atrologicum

This revolution in the general portends good unto the native, for the Sun, Lord of the Ascendent in the radix, is in the Ascendent of the revolution, in conjunction of Venus, who is Governess of the tenth house in both figures. The Moon and Jupiter are in trine also, and both in trine to the Sun and Venus, which portends the native to advance in his honour and esteem, and to receive much assistance from persons of eminency and honour, and so to be in better credit and repute than formerly. It is very probable this auspicious revolution might bring on the effects of the Sun to the trine of Jupiter in part. For according to the opinion of that eminently learned knight, Sir Christopher Heydon, the effects of a direction may either be anticipated or continued before or beyond a direction, as things of the same nature shall happen sooner, and so bring them on; or of a contrary nature, shall retard or hinder them.

To return: If the aphorism of J. Schoner be true, *Quando dominus Ascendentis radicis in revolutione a malis aspicitur, significat nato malum secundum naturam planetae qui aspicit* etc. 'When the Lord of the Ascendent of the radix shall be evilly aspected in the figure of the revolution, it portends evil to the native according to the nature of the planet afflicting'. If it be true (I say), then certainly it will be also true, that when the Lord of the Ascendent is in a revolution well beheld, it shall denote good unto the native from persons or things signified by the planets so beholding him. As for instance, here both the Fortunes and the Moon also befriend the Sun by their amicable beames. Hence it will follow that the health, joy, and good constitution of this native's body and minde, his dignity, honour and estimation (before spoken of) will be the greater. And as Venus is Lady of the fifth, and posited in the horoscope, so the native may have or take much pleasure and delight in his children. He may also have many missives or embassies this year from forraign princes etc., for the fifth house, and the Governour or Governours thereof, hath signification of such.

The position of Jupiter in the fourth (so aspected as before) denotes much advantage and good success unto the native in cities, towns, houses, castles, inheritances and the like; as the last yeer it fell out when Venus was therein. But this not to succeed without much treachery and baseness, and sometimes some kind of loss both of men and treasure, for Saturn, Lord of the second, is in the fourth retrograde, thence casting a square to the second house. The South Node in the third argues much prejudice and unhappiness to the native from or by means of some of his kindred or neerest friends; some discoveries made of his designs by some interception of letters etc. And discontent and trouble in his journeys and removals.

The native was very healthful, pleasant and of good constitution this yeer; gained much honour and estimation, assembled a Parliament at

Nativity of the Late King Charles

Oxford, and was much honoured and renowned by them. He received much honour and content in his children this yeer; two of his sons commenced Doctors of the Civil Laws and Physick in Oxford; and he had a daughter born unto him. There came embassadours unto him, both from France and Holland. He had great success in taking and garrisoning of towns etc. As Harwarden, Arundel, Beecton, Hopton, Warder and Sturton castles; Laply, Grafton, Crew and Borstal houses; took Bolton in Lancashire, and relieved Basing, Banbury and Dennington etc. But he had some losses herewith, as Arundel and Tong castles. And for a verification of treachery and unhappiness by his kindred, Duke Hamilton was now discovered about some trayterous design and sent prisoner to Pendennis accordingly.

On June 29 was the fight at Cropredy Bridge. Some say the Parliament had the better, others the King. Now I know that Saturn the very day of the engagement was on the place of Jupiter in this revolution, and Mars in Taurus in the tenth of the radix. And the Sun and Saturn were in square (which was one good argument that they should fight), but seriously I much question whether either side had occasion to boast.

On July 2 was the fight at Marston-Moor. Prince Rupert was General there, and Mars was then in square to his radical place in that Prince's nativity; an unlikely argument that he could have the better.

On July 23 York was yeelded to the Parliament, and the Sun and the Moon were in conjunction in this native's twelfth house.

On September 1 and 2, the Earl of Essex was worsted in the west. First day the Moon was in trine to the Sun, Lord of the Ascendent of the radix; second day, the Moon in trine of Jupiter, Venus, and Mercury; and Venus and Mercury in the radical place of Jupiter; which were eminent arguments of the victory then obtained by this native.

But now for a further testimony of this native's prejudice from his kindred or relations etc, besides Duke Hamilton's discovery; – the Scots are now come into England against him, although they are his native countrey-men. And for his discontents in journeys and removals, let the hard marches he underwent now be remembered; being pursued by Sir William Waller the Parliament's General, who about this time was reported to go a-King-catching; that he was prejudiced by the interception of letters, let the execution of Kniveton and others make good, who were his supposed spies.

Nativity of the Late King Charles

The Dragon's Tail's no planet, yet it is
In mischief worser than the worst (I wis).

Revolutio Solis ad punctum Radicis,
November 19. 1 hour 54 minutes P.M. 1644.

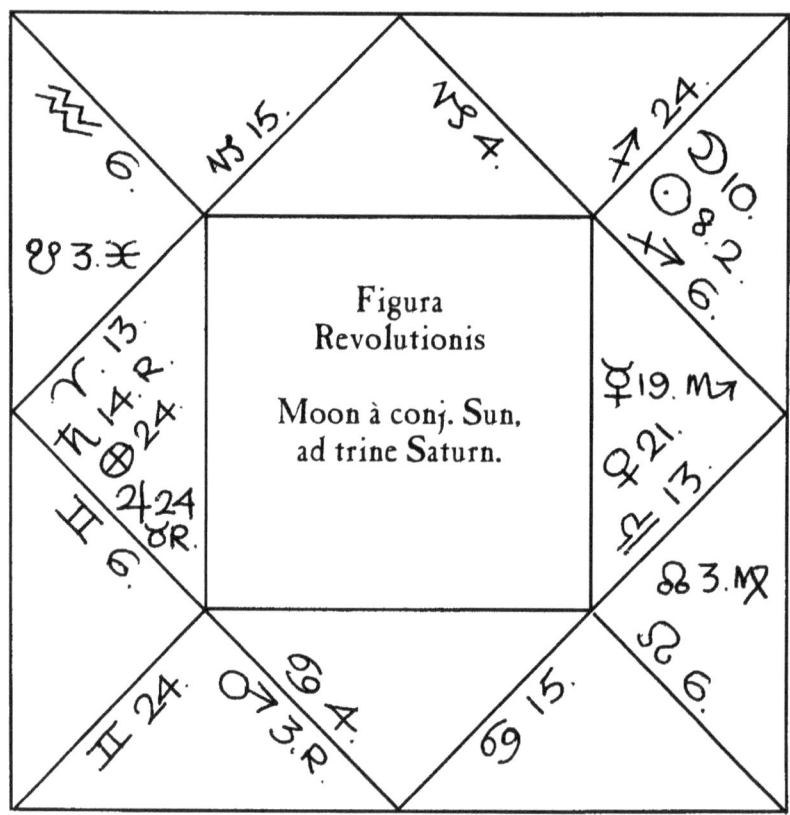

Asc. and Sun ad T.Mars.
Fortuna ad Term Saturn.
Sun ad Trine of Jupiter.

Judicium Astrologicum

These are the directions that happen this yeer; but the later of them is the most remarkable. For astrologers hold that the Sun to the trine of Jupiter portends much honour and renown to the native, be he of what condition he will; but more especially in the geniture of a Prince. Take the testimony of Origanus, fol.746 *de Effectib*. – Sun *ad* trine Jupiter, *Nato confert astutiam, solertiam et ad honores evectionem; unde vel primarius Regis aut magni viri preses efficietur, eritque in sua familia quasi Rex, et passim a potentioribus amabitur etc*. (For you must know that directions operate according to the capacity or condition of the native, and not in all persons alike). It is true, as Origanus saith, in the general, that this direction hath many admirable significations, but their glory will be much abated by the directions hapning in Capricorn, the fall of Jupiter and a sign contrary to his own nature; besides Jupiter is but weak in the radix, namely in Virgo his detriment, and Lord of the eighth house also.

But did there happen nothing of all this, but that the direction had fell in the most happy place of Heaven that could be, and Jupiter a promiser of much good in the radix also (which here he is not), yet the other two directions, namely Ascendent and Sun to the terms of Mars, would very much cloud, if not quite darken the Sun-shine of its eminent portends; for they presage much trouble to the native in the management of everything. Many crosses and contradictions in all his negotiations inclines him to rash actions, and hardly any thing he undertakes hath good success. Besides, you may remember that I shewed in the yeer last past, how that the Sun *ad* trine Jupiter, had (in some respect) been propitious to the native.

The yeer began happily with this native, for he is courted by Commissioners from Ireland and an Embassadour from Spain. The Parliament send proposals to him, are willing to agree; a Treaty is concluded on, the place Uxbridge – all of which were arguments of the Sun *ad* trine Jupiter. But mark the event: the Treaty comes to nothing, it was appointed at an ill time, namely on January 30 and at 5 hours 30 minutes P.M. it began. Now the other directions interpose.

When directions are equal in significations, both good and bad, it is requisite we see which way the revolution bends, for according to the force of that, the native's fate will be byassed.

In the revoutional figure we have Aries the day-house of Mars ascending, and Saturn retrograde therein, in square of Mars his dispositor from the fourth, being retrograde and in detriment also. Which mindes me of an aphorism of that famous physitian and philosopher Andr. Argolus – *In Ascendente revolutionis infortunata, vel in signis ascendens aspicientibus, significat impedimentum, et tristitias de natura ipsius infortunae, et signi in quo fuerit* etc. – That is, 'when Infortunate planets shall be posited in the Ascendent of a revolution, or in signs (evilly) beholding the same, they portend sorrow, grief, and impediment unto the native according to the nature of the afflicting planet or planets, and of the sign or signs in which they shall be posited'.

Saturn and Mars are here the afflicting planets and they are posited in cardinal signs; one being Lord of the seventh in the revolution, the other of the same house in the radix; which very aptly denote that the native's enemies will (this year) do him great prejudice. And as in the two former yeers he gained much by things of the fourth house, namely castles and strongholds, it being then fortified; by the same rule it being now infortunated, (and that doubly) he will be subject to loose as much, if not more, than in both the former yeers he gained. Besides, Venus Lady of the seventh is far stronger than Mars Lord of the Ascendent, she being in her own house and he in his fall retrograde, and falling cadent. The Moon also coming to the radical place of the Sun, and both in the eighth house, encreases the evils and shews many conspiracies and secret connivances to be set on foot to subvert the hopes and happiness of the native; and this from men in power and in eminent places.

Nor does the opposition of Jupiter and Mercury from fixed signs any other than help onward the aforesaid malicious significations, occasioning much treachery to the native from persons about him.

True it is, this was a yeer most unfortunate and unsuccessful and this kingly native did prosper but poorly in his whole affairs. For this yeer, namely on June 14, was the fatal Battel of Nasby, Mars being then on his Ascendent; and both luminaries neer the place of Mars in this figure, and Saturn on the Midheaven of the radix.

Sir Thomas (now Lord) Fairfax was chosen the Parliament's General on December 31, upon such a time that had he been to have warred against the most potent princes in the world, he might according to Art have proved in his attempts an 'Alexander'; but beyond all peradventure he must have proved a victor over this native. For at the time of his election there hapned a trine of the Sun and Jupiter, and the Sun was then in square to the Ascendent of the native's (this yeer's) revolution. To be brief, after this eminent person took his commission and began to act, the native never prospered. For after the fatal Battel of Nasby (for so it may be termed) he endured many hard marches to and again, until at the last, namely on September 24, 1645, he was engaged by his enemies at Routon Heath in Cheshire, at which time the Sun was in opposition to the Ascendent of his Revolution, and Saturn retrograde upon his M.C. in opposition to Mars in the fourth house. The Treaty at Uxbridge (as I told you before) came to nothing; some judged it contrived so on purpose (but I much question the power of man in such things) and that, as well by the ministers of the gospel, as other ministers and agitators in the business. Master Christopher Love, a Presbyterian minister, was noted a great man in these matters, and accordingly in a sermon at Uxbridge discovered himself; yet some few yeers after was beheaded for adhering to the very thing he then was an enemy unto; which was wittily reported on his memory by Mr Rich. Fitz-Smith in his *Ephemeris* for 1654 thus –

> Had one told Love, when (in his heat and passion),
> He thundred for a bloody Reformation;
> (Or when at Uxbridge-Treaty, he did ring
> That fieiry-pulpit-peal against the King)
> His own desires should bring him to the Block,
> Surely he had accounted it a Mock.

Nor was this native free from the jealousie and fear of some persons about him, for (upon information) divers were put in prison by reason of false play. And indeed the later part of this yeer was most obnoxious unto him; he was hunted about very strangely; and so we must be content to leave him in the very midst of his hazzards and dangers.

Nativity of the Late King Charles

Revolutio Solis ad punctum Radicis,
November 19, 1645. 7 hrs 42 m. P.M.

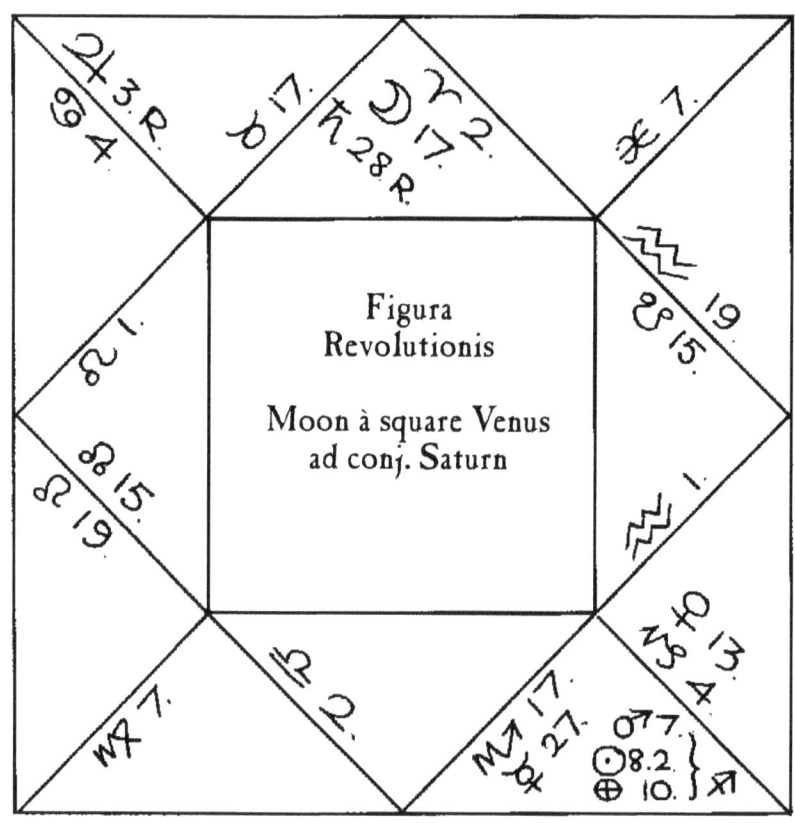

M.C. *ad* opposition, Venus (*cum and sine*) Lat. Arcus direct. 44d. 39m.

	A.D.H.
44d. give	44 234 13
39m.	0 240 21
	44 475 10
Subtract	0 365 0
Time of commencement.	45 110 10

Which happens on March 9, 1646. What it portends we shall have occasion to speak of anon.

Nativity of the Late King Charles

Judicium Astrologicum.

The last yeer was not so inauspicious, but this is probable to prove more unhappy. For directions, transits, and the revolution, are averse unto the native's good. The direction of the M.C. to the opposition of Venus, (drawn forth as you see before) denotes many complexities, infortunacies, griefs and troubles. It makes shipwrack of the native's honour, credit and estimation and abates much of his greatness and dignity, as is apparent by Venus (who is the promittor) her being Lady of the tenth in the radix. And she being in the sixth of the revolution (and the twelfth house of the radix ascending therein) doth very well portend many griefs and dolours, and in plain terms restraint or captivitie; and this the more significantly appears from Venus her being in square of Saturn and the Moon, in the tenth house. It declares also (for the direction is very malicious in many things) a consumption or scattering of the native's riches and estate, and much loss and detriment in his patrimonie, for Venus is governess of the fourth in this figure.

These predictions are notably and most remarkably verified in the grand catastrophe this kingly native now suffered. For his honour and estimation is unhappily (about this time) clouded; he requires a Treaty, the Parliament denies it him; he craves the liberty of coming to London; his desires are therein rejected, and to his dishonour the Great Seal of England is broken and defaced. He now lost many of his garisons; his armies enforced to disband under Prince Rupert and the Lord Hopton etc. The Lord Jacob Ashley is beaten and quite routed neer Stow in the Old.

And he fell so fouly under the frowns of fortune about this time, that his afflictions began to grow too heavie for him, and (without a fortnight or some such time, after the M.C. *ad* opposition Venus directly touched) he left Oxford in disguise, having first ordered the disbanding of his armies and dismantling his garisons, and casts himself upon the Scotch armie, and they detain him prisoner. Which restraint is well signified by these additional arguments besides what was before mentioned, namely Mars his coming to the places of the Sun and Mercury, which according to Origanus prenotes – *Tristicium, labores, ac infirmitates calidas minaecur. Et vel oddides, aut occidetur, si suerit in signo violento vel communi, vel ad mortem esque laboravit.*– Indeed this was a sad yeer unto him and from the very time of his first going to the Scots army he might plainly have seen his death or destruction visible before him.

Nor doth his this yeer's sorrows end here; he is afflicted and troubled, for the sorrows and suffering of his children (for they lie subject to many misfortunes now) as Mars afflicting the Lord of the Ascendent in the fifth house declares. The Prince of Wales is by the Parliament invited to London; he refuses their offer and goes to the Isle of Garnsey, and so for France. The Duke of York's servants are discharged, and the yeer ends with much infortunacie.

Revolutio Solis ad punctum Radicis,
November 19, 13 hours 31 minutes P.M. 1646.

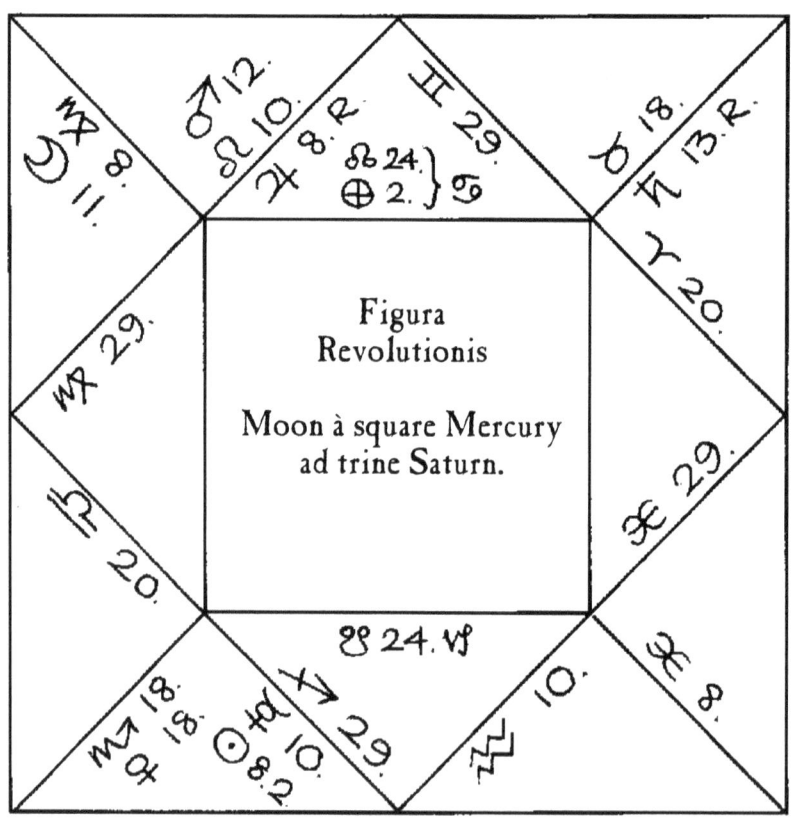

Ascendent and C.A. Moon by direction.

Nativity of the Late King Charles

Judicium Astrologicum.

Venus being principal Governess of the Ascendent in this figure, (there being but one degree of Virgo left to ascend) and she in opposition of Saturn, and square of Mars, and Saturn retrograde upon the Midheaven of the radix, argues many notable designs against the honour, eminencie and power of the native, and these to be carried on with great zeal, affection, and revolution, and yet with much policie. Nevertheless, the native will have many offers and fair shews of friendship and assistance from many, and those very eminent: for the Moon Lady of the tenth is in trine of Saturn, and Mars and Jupiter both in trine to him also, and that from the cusp of the house of friendship. But the Moon being in square to the Sun and Mercury, and Saturn in opposition to Venus, and Mars in square to her (as before) argues all those shews of assistance and offers of friendship and service will not prove either so weighty or worthy as pretended. Yet it's probable they may work much upon this native by reason of the aforesaid testimonies of friendship, and the Moon her being in sextile to Venus Lady of the Ascendent upon the cusp of the third house, might seem to promise some such thing, by the means of some journey or progress. But Saturn and Mars destroys all the hopes thereof (as was noted before) for Mars being Lord of the seventh prenotes much prejudice to happen to the native therein by Martial men, or men in great power and authority; and Saturn argues much mischief to happen by the close and secret counsels (I was about to say conspiracies, for Saturn is in the eighth house) of his publique adversaries, because he is Lord of the seventh of the radix.

Besides all this we finde the Lady of the tenth in the twelfth of the figure, and in square to the Sun and Mercury; which tells us the native's honour and renown is under hatches, and that is likely to be a great abatement of his esteem and credit, both in the minde of souldiers and the vulgar sort of people; for Saturn is the patron of such. Cardinal signs possessing the Angles of the figure, declare the actions of this yeer to be superlatively strange and remarkable, but still for the worst – The South Node, Dragon's Tayl, in the fourth is an argument that the yeer shall end most unfortunately in every thing, unto all which evils the Ascendent to the C.A. of the Moon augments.

It was this yeer that the Scots armie sell their King for moneys, and on February the 17th the armie carryed him prisoner to Holmby House in Northamptonshire, the Sun being then in square to his radical place, and Saturn upon the M.C. of the radix, and there he remained until June 4. At which time Cornet Joyce with a party of horse took him thence at unawares – Jupiter was in square to the tenth of his radix, and the Moon was in opposition to Saturn and Mercury, and in square of Mars, Mars having lately passed his Ascendent. And from that time he was hurryed away to divers places until at length he was brought to Hampton Court neer London, but finding opportunity (though an ill one) namely on November the 11th, he fled thence to the Isle of Wight with Legg and Ashburnham; is there confined by Colonel Hamond, Governour thereof. And thus ended the actions of this yeer; onely take notice, this native made his escape upon an opposition of the Sun and Saturn and could therefore reap no advantage thereby, considering the maliciousness and evil import of the revolution.

Judicium Astrologicum. [See Chart on page 67, opposite]

There are now beginning to operate two directions of evil consequence, namely M.C. *ad* T. Mars, and the Ascendent *ad* square Mars. But these not taking their full effect this yeer but directly happen in the former part of the next, I shall take the lesser notice of them here, and shall chiefly adhere to the testimonies of the revolutional figure for signification of this yeer's actions. Were it not for the prejudice threatned by the two directions (now) coming on, the native might have expected a moderate yeer of this. For this revolutional figure affords us several good testimonies, namely Jupiter neer his radical place and in the ninth house of the figure, which seems to portend some kinde of honour and esteem, and an encrease of reputation from or by the means of persons signified by the ninth house, and Jupiter there; namely churchmen, lawyers, judges, senators etc., and argues the native to receive some kinde of good from them, and that they or some of them should stickle highly for his interest and happiness. But Jupiter being weak, and in square to the Sun Lord of the Ascendent of the radix and to Venus Lady of the seventh, are plain testimonies that the native's hopes and the desires and designs of his friends may meet with some unexpected

Nativity of the Late King Charles

Revolutio Solis ad punctum Radicis,
November 19, 1647. 19 hours 20 minutes P.M.

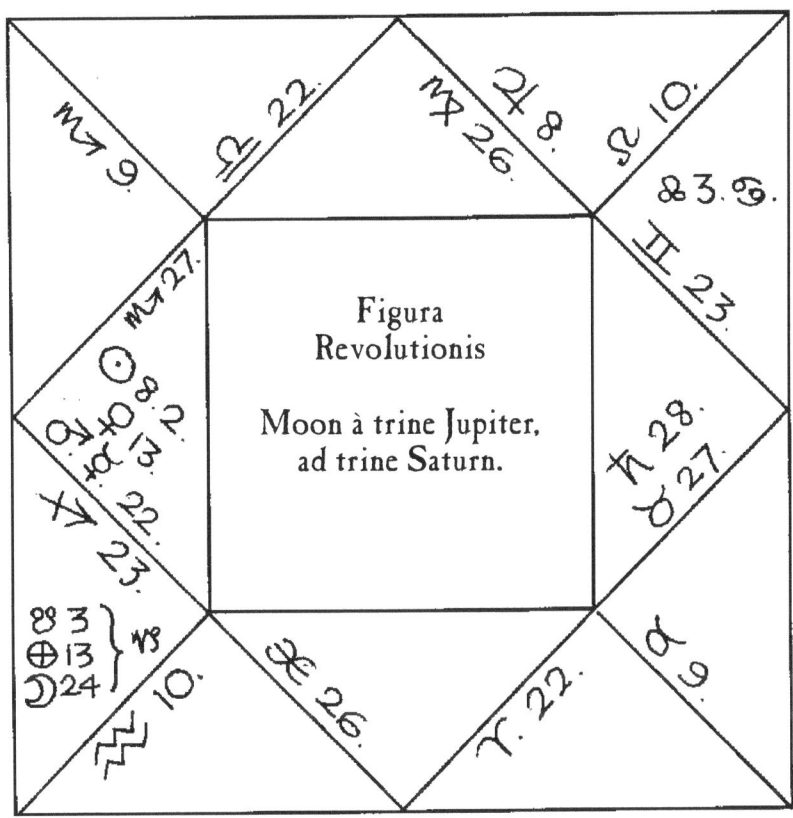

rubbs, obstructions, and difficulties. Nevertheless, Jupiter having great dignities in the Ascendent of this figure, and in trine to the M.C. of the radix, argues the native to acquire something of signal honour and concernment, from or by means of such kinde of persons as were before mentioned, and that his affairs should be put into a better posture and condition than formerly. And this seems to be very well seconded by the Moon's trine to Saturn, and her reception with him by house and exaltation, as if there were a probability of reconciling all differences between this native and his enemies. And Mercury *ad Locum veneris*, gives him the greater hopes that all things will succeed well. But –

  Let no man say
  Before the Ev'ning's come, 'tis a fair day.

For after all these testimonies of a glorious Sunshine, we finde these following arguments of a storm; namely Mercury his being upon the radical place of Venus is rancountred by Mars his position there, which maliciously obscures the good presages thereof; and the good and happy portents of Jupiter are contradicted by Sun, Venus, Mars and Mercury, their squares to him. And the reception of the Moon with Saturn and their square also is lesned by the position of Venus so neer the Scorpion's heart, and the Sun, Mercury and Mars; which seems very much to heighten the spirits and resolutions of his enemies.

All which demonstratively prove – That the faithful aimes and endeavours both of this native himself, and his friends and assistants, will be overruled by the policie and power of his enemies, and that the altitude of his hopes shall be brought low by them. And if we shall speak *ad personas* to the persons of his enemies, we may directly conclude them to be the masters of the sword or pen because Mars and Mercury are the afflicters. And indeed they are the most prodigious enemies that are, (for under them, both the hand and brain are employed) and therefore the greater to be feared.

But besides these, we have the South Node, *Cauda*, in the second house, which (as Schoner saies) much wastes and consumes the estate and treasure of the native. His words are these: *Cauda Draconis in secunda, semper assert damna et difficultates in divitiis.*

The yeer did begin a little cloudily, for within two months of the revolution, namely on January 11th, the Parliament and Army make it the basis of their endeavours to settle the native without the King. But the Moon being then upon the place of Venus in the radix, argued this their design to remain but a little time; for about June following the Parliament themselves began to struggle, and considering of the way they were taking, begin to call the votes (for no further addresses to the King) into question, and think it very convenient to null them by a vote of greater power, which thing they did accordingly. Then they begin to make great preparation for a Treaty with the King, deeming that both the safest and securest course that can be taken for the cure of these bleeding nations. This was fully agreed on, and the day of its commencement, Munday September 18th; the place, Newport in the Isle of Wight. It began at a most infortunate time. Observe the position of heaven thereat.

Nativity of the Late King Charles

The Treatie at the Isle of Wight

Here the Sun is upon the radical place of the Moon, neer the body of Venus, which gave this native great hopes of a good issue. But the Moon being *vacua cursi*, void of course, and afterward applying to a square of the malignant planet Saturn, whose radical place ascends in the figure, and the tenth house of this nativity desends; Saturn retrograde upon the eleventh house of the nativity, and in the eighth of this figure – all which testimonies were averse and contrary to this native's hopes and expectations. It is most sufficiently known that the Treaty came to no good end, although the morning or beginning thereof was cleer and glorious, and promised very fair.

Some bright and splendid mornings vanish soon;
And leave behinde a dismal afternoon!

Nativity of the Late King Charles

However 'tis an argument strong enough to prove the force and power of the revolution in testimonies of a probable good, although it did not long continue as was plainly evidenced by the after arguments.

Nor did this native's evils end here, for lo! he lost all the hopes and expectations he had of the forces in Kent and Essex, and of the Scots which then came into England under the conduct of Duke Hamilton, who were on August 17 defeated at Preston in Lancashire by the valour and power of Oliver Cromwell, late Lord Protector of England etc, then Lieutenant-General of all the Parliament's forces. When the Scots were routed, and all the other weak and vain hopes of this kingly native vanished, the Treaty begins to break off; no agreement ever like to be. The Army then at Windsor agree of a large remonstrance; November 16 just upon a square of the Sun and Mars, and on November 20th present the same to the Parliament, wherein the native is termed the capital offender, and the only Achan that troubled England.

Divers papers and petitions from all parts came both to Parliament and Army, all pretending for the peace of the nations. And lest these should not work their effects or bring about the desired ends of their projectors, many pretended prophets appear, and these have Messages from the Lord to deliver to the chief of the (then) Parliament and Army. The Presbyterians whine it out unlawful and not becoming the saints and servants of God to make peace with the wicked; but afterward change their notes. All which things proved a delay to this native's designs, and were well signified by the position of Mars and Mercury upon the place of Venus, who was Lady of the tenth in the radix.

Thus did this yeer's actions receive an end; but himself still remaining in *Salva Custodia* at and during the pleasure of the Parliament and Army.

Judicium Astrologicum. [Chart on page 71, opposite]

Although it was not less than an oraculous speech of this kingly native, which he uttered in his meditations on death after the votes of non-addresses and upon his closer imprisonment, namely – THERE ARE FEW STEPS BETWEEN THE PRISONS AND THE GRAVES OF PRINCES; yet, that it may most eminently appear, the greatest acts and accidents, even of the highest as lowest persons in the world, are

Nativity of the Late King Charles

Revolutio Solis ad punctum Radicis,
November 19, 1 hour 9 minutes P.M. 1648.

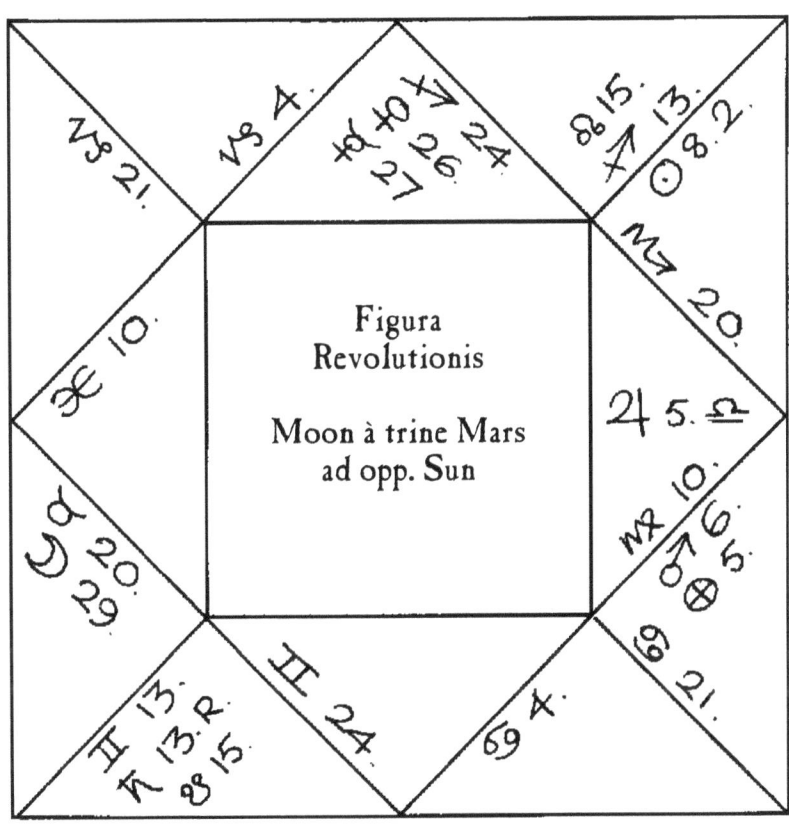

written in indelible letters in the HEAVENS, and there plainly to be read by persons learned in the language of that glorious Book. You may observe that the Ascendent, who was hylech, or giver of life in this Prince's nativity, is directed to the malicious quadrate of Mars, who is the abscissor or destroyer thereof. Hear Origamus on the effects of such a direction – *Minatur etiam pericula corporis, casum ex alto, vulnera, ferri adustiones et dispendia non modica. Ut vero nato inimicos suscitat - accusationes, moves et iram, violentos ac temerarios impetus in nato accendit: Ita simul admonet, ut toto tempore directionis, bellicos conflictus fugiat, et loca, in quibus tormentales machinae ejiciuntur, ne subita morte e viventium, numero tollatur* etc. – Those that have a desire to know the English

Nativity of the Late King Charles

thereof may observe what follows in the verification; or if they shall desire to know what the words mean they may finde that in my *Doctrine of Nativities*, fol.184, part 1.

But besides this, the eighth house of the radix is horoscopical in the revolution, and the Sun Lord of the Ascendent of the radix, is in the eighth house of this figure; and there happens an eclipse of the Moon in Gemini the very day of the revolution of this yeer; all which most plainly portended his death.

This yeer began as the last ended, yet the Sun being in sextile to Jupiter, and Jupiter in the Moon's place, gave the native a little hopes, though but weak, by reason of the Sun his position in the eighth house, namely the most malicious place in the whole heavens. That had its explanation in the Parliament's voting this kingly native's concessions satisfactory, and by the Dutch endeavouring his safety.

But alas! what avails so small a glimmering of hopes when the person hoping is threatened by so thundering a direction? For now on December the first the Army take him away from the Isle of Wight, at which time Mars was in opposition to the Ascendant of his this yeer's revolution.

Then on January 4 the Supreme Authority of England etc. is voted in the Commons of England etc. and this native deprived of all his honour, power and dignity. Saturn Lord of the seventh of the radix was then in square to the Sun and the Moon opposing the Ascendent, and in square to the tenth house.

On January 20th he was brought before a High Court of Justice the first time; the Moon then upon the place of Mars in the revolution, and Mars retrograde upon the radical place of Jupiter, and the Moon then applying to a square of Saturn, opposite Venus, and conjunct of Mars.

And on January 27th he was sentenced to death; the Moon then being upon the places of the Sun and Mercury, in square of Mars, who was in quartile to the Sun's radical place.

But upon January the 30th he dyed; at which time Saturn, Lord of the seventh, was stationary upon the place of the Moon in this revolution, and opposite place of the Sun. And the Sun upon the cusp of the seventh house of the radix, the better to illustrate the setting or departure of (him whom divers lamenting called him after his death) the brightest Sun that ever ruled the day of Great Britain's Peace, from the Conquest unto his time!

Nativity of the Late King Charles

It is observable that Saturn, Lord of the seventh of the radix, was in opposition to the place of the Lord of the Ascendent thereof, namely the Sun, from the day of his revolution to the day of his death.

Behold with what aspect the heavens view'd the Earth in the latitude of London (the place where he suffered) at the time of his expiration.

Thus fell this (once) most stately cedar! who while he lived, was the subject of his people's hate; but dead, lamented by his most professed enemies.

– *Certa stant omnia lege*.

The highest Monarch, and the loftiest State,
In all things yeilds unto the Laws of Fate.

FINIS

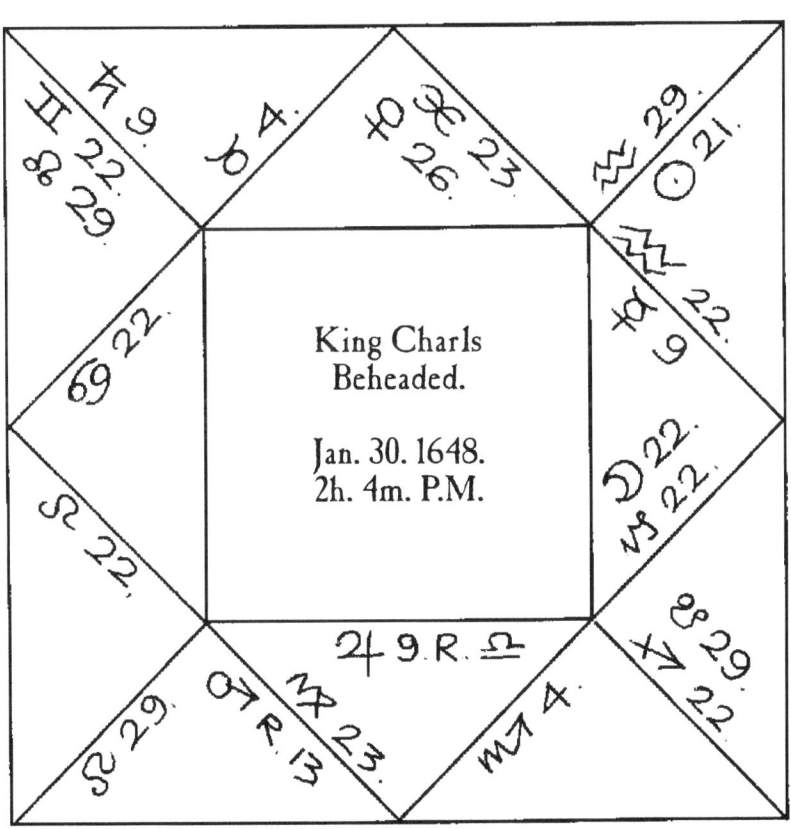

AN
APPENDIX
to the fore-going
GENITURE.

For the advantage and encouragment of the ingenious student, I shall here (having the opportunity of the press) impart a secret in art unto him, and that not inconsiderable, which if it be once thoroughly and truly understood will sufficiently acquaint him with the true reasons in art of the adverse and happy fates of persons as they stand related unto each other, either by birth, dealing or friendship. For from a certain concatenation of celestial or superior causes (*sub Deo*) which are onely to be seen in the roots of the nativities of persons, do all disastrous and happy fates proceed. From that fountain alone springs all sympathy and antipathy, and men do either cross or crown each other's actions, as their genitures do either accord or disagree.

But because I would not impose upon the belief or opinion of men, (as many strange writers in these days do!) without the warrant of good authority or reason; we are taught by the learned Ptolemy in his *Quadrip. lib.4 cap.7.* how to discern the natural sympathy or disagreement between ourselves and others; and this alone from the harmony, or discord, of the genitures of both. The fame-learned authour in his *Cent. Aphor.33.* tells us – *Amor odiumque tum ex luminarium concordia discordiaque tum ex utriusque genitur a ascenentibus deprehenditur, et.* That is, 'from the agreement or disagreement of the luminaries, and the Ascendents of the nativities of two, is cleerly discovered the love or hate that shal happen between them'.

Now we are to understand that there is an accidental, as well as essential love or hatred between persons; whence many times it cometh to pass, they are friends and enemies to each other unknown, or at unawares. As for instance a man may accidentally, or against his will, kill his friend, (as Mintor his Aspatia in the Tragedie), or do him or them, other less hurt or prejudice. And this peradventure when as he purely intendeth safety and good unto him. But this antipathy being accidental and casual, and not very customary or common, it is the less minded, not only by the generality of men, but many times neglected by artists.

And so on the contrary, a man that is naturally and avowedly an absolute enemy to another may yet by word or action, before he be aware thereof (for it is no more in man to order his words than steps), prove an eminent friend to the advantage (as it may fall out) either of life, estate, or good name – and yet have no real intent of good toward him at all. As it hapned in the case of Berimbia, whose death was designed by Castabella her sister; yet being discovered by Antonia's servant, both her love, liberty, and preservation were thereby procured and secured. And indeed such accidents are common, though not commonly observed by men. The best philosophy read in the schools takes no knowledge hereof.

But to proceed, the learned Ptolemy goes further and doth not stick at the sympathy or antipathy of persons barely, but acquaints us with the way to discover the kinds of things in which they shall, or shall not agree. – *Concordium inter duos facit conveniens stellarum figuratio, speciem rei significantium ex qua benevolentia in utriusque genitura constituta est.* 'By the convenient configurations or positions of the stars is known the friendship that shall happen between two; but the kinde or quality of the thing in which they agree, or profit or advantage each other, that is known from the constitution of both their genitures'. The same, *mutatis mutandis*, we are to understand of the discord between persons, and the detriment and disprofit they may occasion the one for the other.

The nativity of Maximilianus Stampa, was not very promising of itself unto him, but corresponding and sympathizing with Sforzia's the Duke of Millain, by his means and favour, Stampa attained to very great preferment. And on the contrary, Joshua Silvester, that famous poet, a man of incomparable parts as his learned works testifie, yet having the unhappiness to be *ab origine* antipathetical to King James of England, he could never gain his favour for any Court (or other) preferment. And so, notwithstanding his many and excelling parts, dyed poor.

I know a person (a very good friend of mine) who had as great a pretended friend (*Quoad Capax*) as any the world could boast of; and this not without some merit, for seven yeers together he was as a servant to him, and ventured both his pen, purse and person, for and on his behalf.

Nativity of the Late King Charles

Yet at the length, notwithstanding the great and mountain promises and pretences that eminent pretended friend had made this person spoken of, both he and his pretences vanished on a sudden, without the least iota or mole-hill of performance. Nay, (as my friend hath told me) this pretended friend of his, instead of making good his promises hath done him many superlatively manifest injuries, and those without the least occasion given. Yea, and hath endeavoured his ruine also. Such poysonous snakes do great pretenders prove!

The person acquainting me with this prodigious disaster, procured me also the nativities of both persons. And behold, after some curious and serious observations on them, I found that the great pretended friend had, in his nativitie, Saturn in the very Ascendent of the abused person, and in opposition to the place of the Lord of the Ascendent; and had his Sun in the place of Mars also. All of which were most manifest arguments of essential malice and hatred, although there were never so much love and friendship pretended. But I shall take more peculiar notice of this and other infortunacies, in my intended Book of Genitures.... And so return to my purposed matter.

Setting aside these short instances I have already produced, that my Appendix may be the more pertinent and proper to the geniture preceding, my principal parallel instances shall be in the nativities of several of that eminent native's neerest relations, namely –

1. The nativity of the   Queen Mary.
2.   Prince Charls.
3.   Duke of York.
4.   Duke of Glocester.
5.   Lady Mary.
6.   Lady Elizabeth.
7.   Lady Henrietta.

And this I do, not as if I idolized either any person or family in the world, for I know the breath of a Prince is in his nostrils, as well as that of a Peasant, and there is no salvation in the sons of men! But among the genitures that I have been conversant and studious in, I cannot finde more convenient examples for my present intended purpose than those; for all of them (possibly it may be by reason of their affinity and relation) have been made either happy or unfortunate, as that eminent native's fortune hath either increased or abated.

Nativity of the Late King Charles

SECT. 1. The Geniture of Queen Mary.

This illustrious Lady (a daughter of France) was born in the yeer of our Lord 1609 on November the 26, new stile, 15 hours 2 minutes P.M. afternoon, under the latitude of 49 degrees. The Sun's place unto that moment of time is Sagittarius 5 degrees 1 minute.

	deg.	m.
Right Ascention of Sol	243	4
Right Ascention of time	225	30
Sum of both	468	34
Circle subtract	360	00
Right Ascention of M.C. remains	108	34
Add	90	00
That produces O.A. of the Ascendent	198	34

The Figure of Heaven without farther operation is as followeth [overleaf].

I shall spare to descant much astrologically or otherwise upon the figure of this illustrious geniture; I will only take notice that the fate of this eminent princess was the most kinde unto her, and presaged her to be most happy in her younger yeers, but harsh and cruel beyond measure afterward. And this is plainly seen by the figure before-going, where Venus, Lady of the Ascendent, and the Part of Fortune, are posited in the horoscope; the Dragon's Head in the tenth house, and the benign planet Jupiter locally in the ninth, in trine to the Ascendent. But Saturn and the Dragon's Tail are in the fourth house, and both the luminaries in the third house, in opposition to Jupiter, a fortunate planet, but very weak (otherwise) being both retrograde and in detriment.

That astrologers may see this is the true figure of this eminent Lady's birth, I shall present them with some remarkable accidents which have already hapned unto her, by the which I have corrected it.

1. Aged neer 16 yeers, became Queen of Great Brittain by marriage.
2. Aged 29 and 30 yeers, a dangerous feaver and violent cold, and many scandals, and unhappy suspitions cast upon her honour.
3. Aged 32 yeers, departed from her honour and dignity.
4. Aged neer 34 yeers, the Parliament vote her a traitor.

Nativity of the Late King Charles

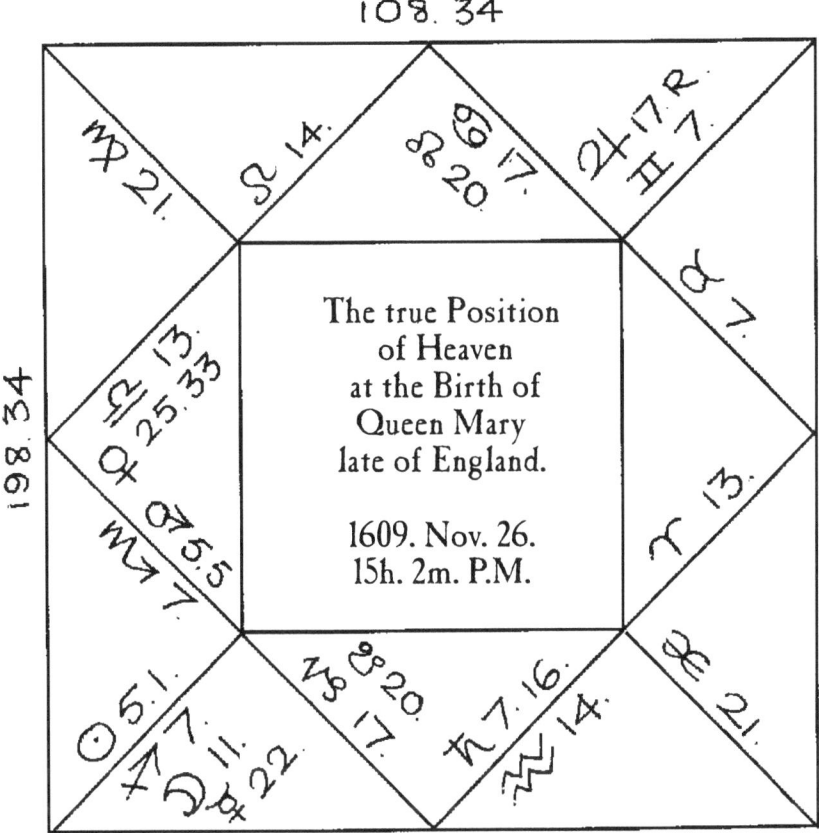

5. Aged 39 yeers, she becomes a widdow, and underwent many griefs and troubles etc.

6. A dangerous flux and fever, being aged 47 yeers.

1. The first accident, namely her honourable marriage, was occasioned by the occurse of the Ascendent to the body of Venus, (the proper Patroness of pleasure and delight), and the Moon's direction to the sextile of Venus, accompanied with the *Medium Coeli* to the trine of the Sun. All of them (in respect of time) hapning very neer together.

But then there hapned also (a little before) the Sun's direction to the opposition of Jupiter; which promittor being weak might very notably denote that in the end a cloud of infortunacie should cover or pass upon the honour and excellencie of that so eminent and remarkable undertaking. If we ask the world, whether this native hath not met with more corrosive than balsam (setting aside the peculiar joyes and blessings of marriage) in that undertaking? It will answer aloud, She hath.

The second, namely the fever, scandals and suspitions etc. To speak to the later first; about the time mentioned, Maria de Medices, the Mother-Queen, came into England, whose coming was the ground of many scandals cast upon this native, and the hard thoughts, suspitions and jealousies contracted against her and her religion; and of the plots, knacks, and contrivances, which were supposed to be of her contriving, framing and projecting. These, I say, together with her fever, and a violent cold, were occasioned by the Ascendent's occurse *ad corp. Martis*, to the body of Mars by direction. Saturn then came to his radical place, transiting the place of the direction by a malicious square all the yeer long. The Sun that yeer was eclipsed in the very degree of the Moon in her radix also.

3. In the yeer 1641, this eminent native departed from her dignity and glory and returned no more unto the same. In her nativity, the Ascendent was directed to the quartile of the cruel planet Saturn, and in her revolution that yeer there was a quartile of Sol to Saturn, and another of Jupiter and Mars. Mars then returned to his own place; Saturn to the quartile of the places of Sol, Jupiter and Luna. The direction, revolution and transits, all most malicious and unfortunate. If the Ascendent to the quartile of Saturn in this nativity were thus mischievous and cruel, what may he hope for that hath his Midheaven directed to the body of Saturn in Leo?

4. In the yeer 1643, and 34th yeer of this native's age, she was very active in procuring assistance, or supplies, for the late King her husband; for which activity the Parliament of England vote her a traytor. The direction before remembred of the Ascendent's quartile to Saturn, she yet laboured under. And Saturn all that yeer transited the opposite place of the Ascendent of the radix, and the quartile of the Ascendent of the revolution too. The Moon also was twice that yeer eclipsed, namely once in the Ascendent of this native's radix, and the second time neer the opposite degree thereof, all which were arguments of much infortunancie. But to signifie her activity before-mentioned, the Midheaven this yeer was directed to the trine of Mercury.

5. This eminent native, about the yeer 1648, being aged 39 yeers, underwent many griefs and perplexities, considering her capacity of birth

etc. She was necessitated to secure herself in France; and at this time also became a widdow. The directions and transits now in force were these: The Moon to the contra-antiscion of Jupiter; the Midheaven to the terms of Mars, to the contra-antiscion of Mars, and to Cor Leonis by direction. In the revolution Saturn was in opposition to the place of the Sun and Moon, and Mars in square to them both.

6. In the yeer 1656 this native was dangerously ill of a violent flux and fever; insomuch that she was (with us in England) often reported to be dead. And some prejudice hapned also to her in estate at that time. The Moon was then directed to a quartile of Venus, Lady of the Ascendent; and the Midheaven to the square of the Sun, and the contra-antiscion of Venus.

Thus was this illustrious geniture rectified. Her most dangerous yeer will be the 56th, for then the Sun will be directed to the square of Venus in the fourth house, neer to the Dragon's Tayl; and she is Governess both of the eighth house and the Ascendent.

Now if we compare this geniture with that kingly one before-going, we shall finde Jupiter in this nativitie in quartile to the places of the Sun, Mercury, Mars and Venus in that, and in square to his own place also. The Moon's Nodes in this are directly contrary to their places in that geniture.

Mars is in this, in the place of Saturn in that; and Saturn here, in square to the cusps of his tenth and fourth houses. All the good that is, is this – The Moon in this geniture is in the place of the Sun in that; and the Moon in that, in the Ascendent of this.

Now, although it be true that these two natives accorded singularly well and were rarely known to differ, as I have at large in the geniture before proved, yet where heaven makes a difference by appointing contrary or different radixes, such persons by their love, friendship and affection do often prove the destruction and ruine of each other insensibly, and against their knowledge, power, inclinations, or desires. And thus much shall serve for this illustrious nativity.

SECT. II. The Nativity of Prince Charls.

I have seen several nativities that have been reported to be this princely native's true one. But one more especially that all our London astrologers rest securely confident is the right, which gives the time of birth to be, in the yeer of our Lord 1630, May the 29, 30 minutes P.M. or after noon. Now we know there can be but one truth; and if this be it, I would willingly demand what directions those are (by such a correction) should signifie these accidents following, which have already hapned unto him? I cannot (by the best of my skill) discover any, and am therefore apt to suspect the verity thereof.

1. Aged 9 yeers, broke his arm, and discrasie in body.
2. Aged 10 yeers, a slight fever, and spice of the jaundies.
3. Aged 12 yeers, the measels, left London etc.
4. Aged 16 yeers, went to France, had a scarlet fever.
5. Aged 20 yeers, crowned in Scotland.
6. Aged 21 yeers, worsted at Worcester.

By the time given, before-mentioned, there is but one of these accidents that can have a direction to signifie it, and that is the crowning of him in Scotland, and that's the Midheaven to the trine of Jupiter. But that is justly liable to suspition, for the M.C. *ad* trine Jupiter, hapning in the house of honour and renown, and in the exaltation of Jupiter, and Jupiter essentially dignified also, should have signified a more lasting and durable honour, than that was to him. Besides, we may suspect it upon this account also; there are no other accidents agree with it. But now by my correction there are directions to signifie all accidents, as I shall plainly make appear.

This illustrious Prince was born (as I have rectified) on May the 29, 1630, 10 hours 21 minutes A.M. *Ante Meridiem*.

	degree	min.
The Sun's place to that time, is	Gemini 17	24
His right Ascention	76	18
Right Ascention of time given	335	15
The sum	411	33
Circle subtract	360	00
R.A. of Midheaven	51	33

Nativity of the Late King Charles

Add the Quadrant	90	00
Oblique Ascention of the Ascendent	141	33

Behold the figure!...

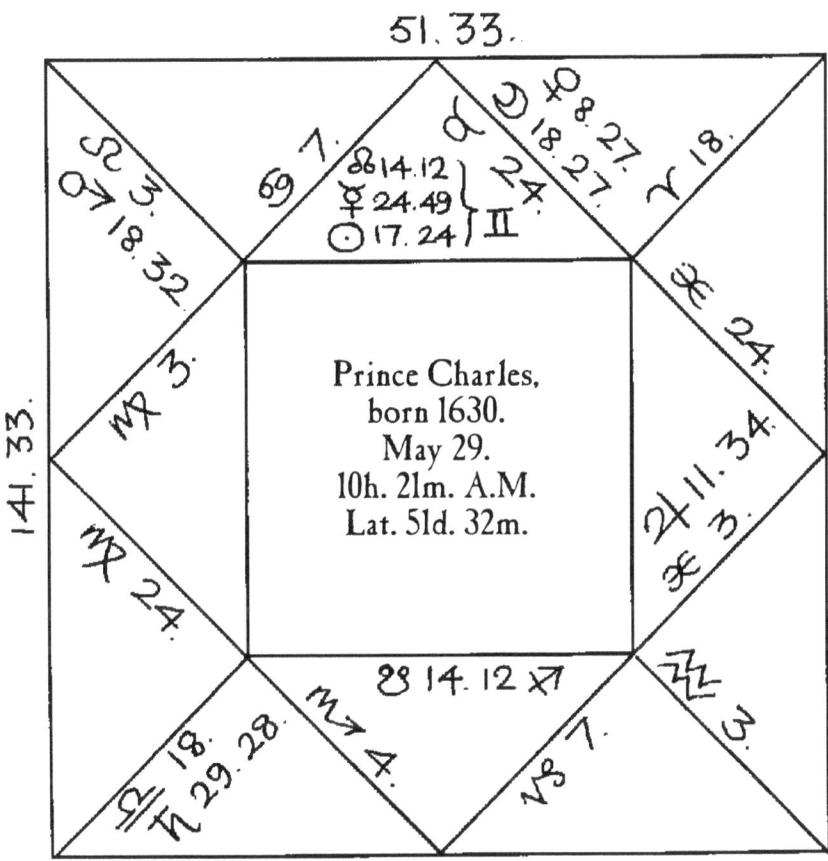

Now observe the verification.

1. Aged about nine yeers, he broke his arm and was sickly etc. Then was the Moon directed to the terms of Mars, and to the Pleiades or Seven Stars, they being of a violent nature, and neer the ecliptique, might very aptly presage those accidents.

2. Being aged ten yeers, this native had a fever and a spice of the jaundies (they are both diseases of Mars); the Sun was then directed to the terms of Mars, neer violent fixed stars. And Mars at that time

was in opposition to the Sun's radical place, and in square also to the Ascendent of the radix. And the Sun and Saturn near that time were conjoyned in the sixth house of the radix.

3. This native about the twelfth year of his age had the measels; he left the City of London with his father and then began his most unfortunate troubles etc. The occasion of which was the direction of the Ascendent to the opposition of Jupiter; and in his revolution for that year were a crowd of mischievous configurations to concomitate it, namely (1) A square of the Sun and Jupiter. (2) A conjunction of Saturn and Mars. (3) A square of the Sun and Saturn. (4) A square of Saturn and Mercury. (5) A square of Mars and Mercury. (6) A square of Saturn and Venus. (7) A square of Mars and Venus, besides the many unfortunate transits that then also happened.

4. In the year 1646 this native left his native country and went to France; he had there a scarlet fever. At that time the Sun was (again) directed to the terms of Mars, and to the stars of Hercules also, in the beginning of Cancer. Saturn at that time passed the place of the Moon in the radix. But Jupiter passing by his eleventh house in trine to his own place, and in sextile to the Moon and Venus, and the Ascendent also, gave him a most friendly reception and entertainment in France.

5. If we may admit reasonably his being crowned King of Scotland into the number of accidents considerable, without offence to any, I shall then say it was not upon the Midheaven to the trine, but square of Jupiter; and perhaps that might be the reason the honour of that action was of so short a duration or continuance. And indeed that direction might go down well enough with some of our astrologers to portend that accident, for it happens from signs of short or oblique ascentions, which they commonly affirm is equivalent to a sextile. But if that were true, yet it hapned in the debilities of Jupiter, namely Gemini. Ergo, the weaker for that.

This direction might also denote (as to his nativity) the death of the King his father, etc. For Sagittarius being wholly intercepted in the fourth house of the nativity, Jupiter (whose quadrate is the promittor in this direction) is the natural significator of his father.

6. When he was aged 21 years, namely in the yeer 1651, he entered England with an army; but was encountered and put to flight by Oliver late Lord Protector of England, then General of the English Forces. The

Nativity of the Late King Charles

Ascendent at that time came to the square of the Sun by direction and Saturn then transited his eleventh house (there destroying his hopes), and Jupiter was in square to the Ascendent of his radix.

The very day of the battel at Worcester, it is observable that the Sun was in quartile to his radical place. Jupiter was in quartile to the Ascendent of the radix *ad gradum*. Mars was in opposition to the place of the Moon and Midheaven; and the Moon in square to Mars and Venus. For the Sun to the trine of Jupiter; that was in force in the yeer 1657 at which time the Spaniard did very much assist him in divers things, but more especially moneys. Some say £100,000.

Thus have I proved this nativity to be the true one, and do commend it to the judgment and scanning of every ingenious artist. And if any such shal find me either too wide or short of the truth in any thing I have here done, I shall most freely and willingly (upon better reasons afforded me than those I have urged) retract this my opinion, and submit to their better judgments.

In the next place, it is requisite that we compare this geniture with that of the late King his father; and then we shall find the Ascendent of that nativity to be the place of Mars in this. Secondly, the Dragon's Tail in this, is upon the place of the Sun in that geniture. Thirdly, the Sun in that geniture was in opposition to the Sun in this. Fourthly, the Sun in this nativity is in quartile to the place of Jupiter in that; and the Lord of the fourth house here, which signifies the father.

All which arguments are transparent and conspicuous enough to signifie the accidental infortunacie that befel this princely native, and to prove him also an equal sufferer in that prodigious misfortune with the King his father, which torrent-like overwhelmed the happiness and honour of that eminent family. I might here have taken notice of his future fate, but this dilemma disswades me.

It must be either Good or Evil ...

If it hap to prove good, my acquainting the world therewith might render me dangerous unto the power that protects me. If it should be bad, my publication thereof would be accounted envy. To avoyd both the horns of this dilemma, I shall acquiesce in what I have done, and leave the rest to be performed by such, that *cum privilegio* may publish any thing. And thus much shall serve for this nativity.

Nativity of the Late King Charles

SECT. 3. The Duke of York's Nativity.

James Duke of York, second son to Charles late King of England, was born in London in the year 1633, the 14th of October, 11h. 30m. P.M.

The place of Sun by calculation is Scorpio	1.	44
His R. Ascention is	209.	34
Right Ascention of time	172.	30
Sum	382.	4
Circle subtract	360.	0
Right Ascention of M.C. remains	22.	4
The Quadrant add	90.	0
Oblique Asc. of the Ascendent	112.	4

The figure of this nativity (without further operation) is as followeth.

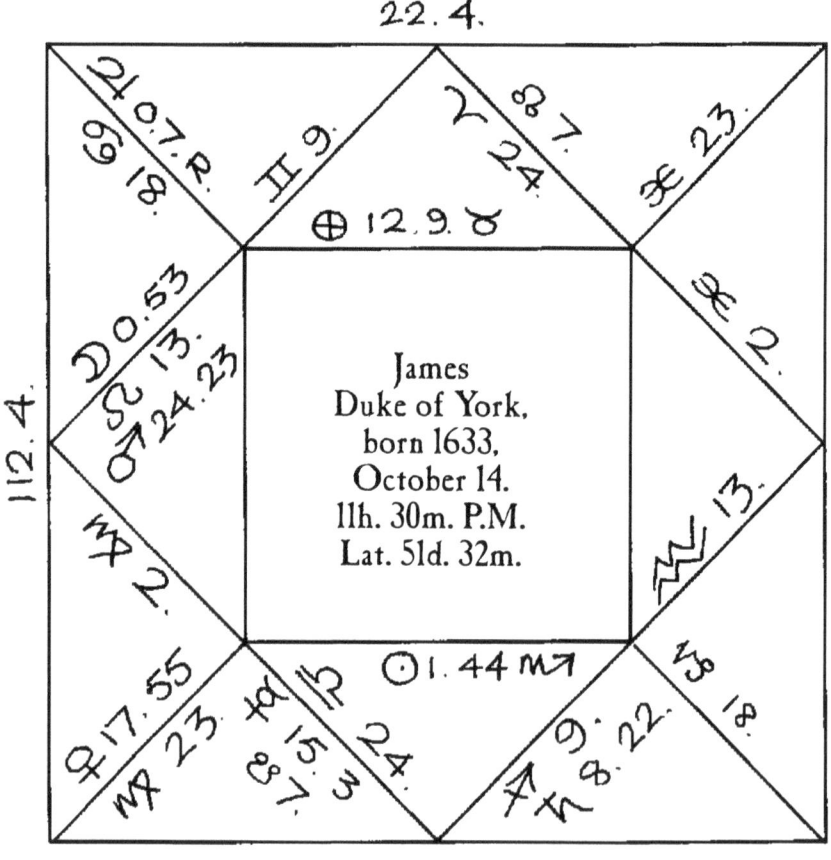

Nativity of the Late King Charles

I have divers nativities which have been said to be this eminent native's true one, but I can put confidence in none but this; and that this is the true one I suppose will appear from the true correction and verification thereof, by the several accidents following.

1. The native about a year and half old, had an imposthume broke in his head, and it continued running near five years together from the time it began. The direction that occasioned this accident was the Moon's occurse to the square of the Sun, who is *Dominus Ascendentis*; and it happening from fixed signes, namely Leo and Scorpio, might well argue the tedious continuance thereof.

2. In the yeer of our Lord 1646, this native had a sharp ague, which continued five weeks upon him. It began in February. In the revolution that yeer there was an opposition of the Sun and Saturn, and this in square to the Moon's radical place. The ponderositie of Saturn shews his transits dangerous.

3. In the yeer 1650, being the seventeenth yeer of his age, the Ascendent came to the body of Mars in a fiery sign, namely Leo; at which time this eminent native underwent the danger and violence of a desperate fever. And he was involved in many other troubles and unhappiness besides.

4. Being 20 yeers of age, namely in the yeer 1653, this princely native was wounded in Flanders, and was also surprised by a fever of which he lay ill a long time. The Sun (namely Lord of the Ascendent) was directed to the hostile beams of Mars his quartile. A most dangerous direction.

5. This native naturally is subject to a weak sight, which seems to be signified plainly by the quartile of the luminaries; the one being neer nebulose or cloudy stars, and the other neer stars of a violent nature – *Erit in visu nati vitium cum* Moon *Soli adversa est, ac Nebulosis stellis conjungitur.* (That is) 'the native's sight will be weak, or vitiated, when the Moon shall be in ill aspect of the Sun; or if she shall be in conjunction with stars that are nebulose or cloudy'. *Ptol. Cent. Aphor.69 Almanser* saith the same in effect, *Aphor.15*.

The yeer 1667 will be a most perillous and dangerous yeer unto him, for then will two violent directions operate together, namely the Moon to the body of Mars in Leo, and the Sun to the body of Saturn

Nativity of the Late King Charles

in Sagittarius. What they both signifie you may read in my *Doctrine of Nativities* lately published, *fol. 193 and 200, in part 1*. They are very dangerous directions.

The testimonies of disagreement between this nativity and the geniture of the late King are chiefly these –

1. The Ascendent of that nativity is the place of Mars in this native's.

2. The Moon in this geniture is upon the very cusp of the twelfth house in that; and in quartile to the place of Saturn in that also.

3. The place of Saturn there, is the place of the Sun here; and the place of Saturn in this, is to a degree the place of the Sun in that radix.

4. The Moon's place in that, is the place of the Dragon's Tail in this. There is nothing of agreement or concordancie between them; but the position of Venus in this nativity, is the place of Jupiter in that. Which you see is counterbalanced by the many contrary arguments before noted. It is therefore no matter of wonder or astonishment to me that this princely native is necessitated to drink deep of the cup of affliction and cross fortune, which was the sad portion of his illustrious father. This shall suffice for arguments of agreement etc., and the nativity itself.

SECT. 4. The Duke of Glocester's Nativity.

Henry Duke of Gloucester, third son to the late King Charles, was born in the year of our Lord 1640, on July 8, 5 hours 45 minutes P.M. afternoon.

	deg.	min.
Locus Sun, *est*	Cancer 26.	18
Ascentio Recta Sun *est*	118.	20
Ascentio Recta Temporis	85.	15
Ascentio Recta Med. Coeli, est	204.	35
Add	90.	0
Ascentio Obliqua Ascendentis	294.	35

The Heavens beheld the Earth as the figure following represents, at the time aforesaid.

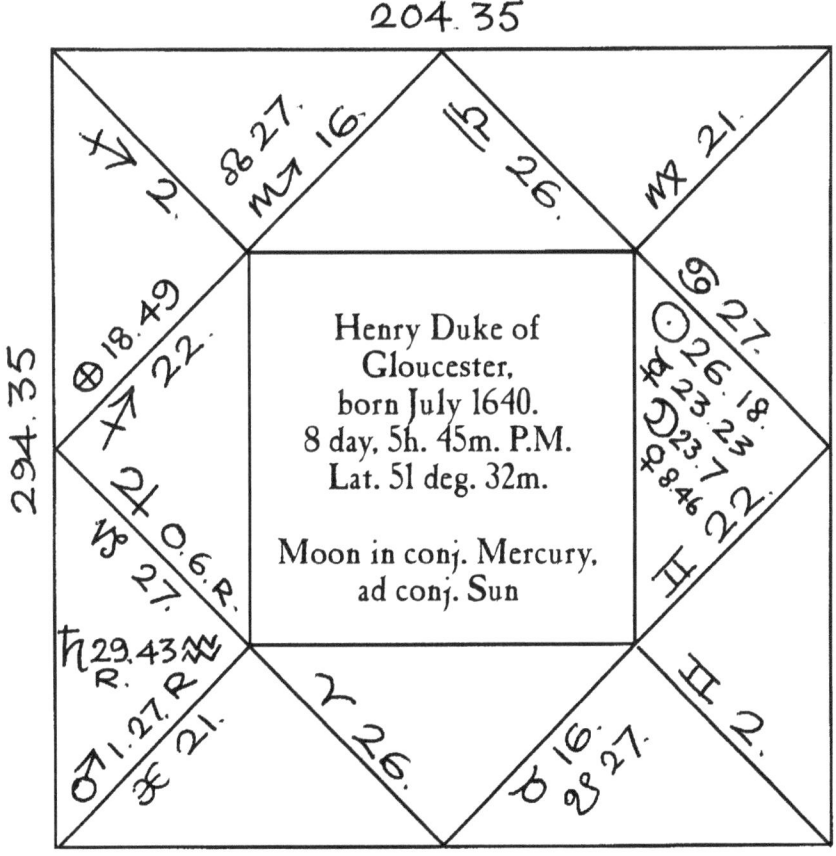

I could never obtain very many accidents that have as yet happened to this native. The most material accident that I have met with is a scarlet fever which happened to this native in the beginning of the year 1643, and it seems very well to accord with the Moon's coming to the body of the Sun by direction, near many violent fixed stars, in Cancer.

If I may take the liberty to speak freely, and according to this art, this geniture is one of the worst that ever I saw, for a native of princely extraction especially, as this eminent person is. For here we find the three superior planets retrograde, and Jupiter Lord of the Ascendent under the earth in Capricorn his fall.

The luminaries are in conjunction (I mean with the moiety of their orbs) combusting Mercury upon the cusp of the eighth house, the most unfortunate place of the whole heavens; and all of them are in square to the cusp of Dignity. The fortunate planets are in opposition from Angles, and the unfortunate are in conjunction in the second house of the figure. I spare to urge the aphorisms authors afford us for the true understanding of such positions, because I do not intend the exact and copious calculation of this nativity, as I have done the King's, his father.

In the 26 year of this Prince's age, there happens two very good directions, namely Medium Coeli to the trine of the Moon, and to the trine of Mercury. But the 31 or 32 years, in all humane probability, will prove very dangerous, if not fatal, unto him; for then the Ascendent (which is hylech here) comes to the oppositions of both the luminaries and Mercury.

True it is, the Midheaven at the same time comes to a trine of the Sun etc., but the Sun being locally and virtually in the eighth house, and the directions before remembred falling in Capricorn, the detriment of the Moon, who is here anareta; I see not in reason how the fury portended can be wholly anticipated by the Midheaven's occourse to the trine of the Sun. It is very probable that such a direction may meliorate or better the condition of the native under two such cruel ones, until the fatal approach; but without all controversie, these directions cut off Life. For when killing directions happen, all the assistance a good one can do, is by interposition to stave their fury off for a time; but it cannot wholly prevent their dire effects.

Nativity of the Late King Charles

Here seems to be no extraordinary discord between this native's radix and his princely father's nativity. The worst that is, here is a conjunction of Saturn and Mars in this nativity, in opposition to the Ascendent of that, and in square to the place of the Sun also.

But then, to make amends for it, here is for the Ascendent of this nativity, the very degree of Venus in that. The figures themselves are in trine to each other. The luminaries in this are in friendly sextile to the place of Jupiter in that geniture, though not to the degrees exactly. And thus much may serve for this nativity.

SECT. 5. The Nativity of the Lady Mary.

This illustrious Princess, eldest daughter to the late King, was born in the year of our Lord, 1631, upon November 4, 7 hours 10 minutes *Ante Meridiem*, or before noon, in London.

The place of the Sun to that *punctum temporis*, is (by the Astronomical Tables in my *Doctrine of Nativities*) in Scorpio 21 degrees 40 min. For the planets' places I follow that excellent Ephemeridist-Master, David Origanus; and the Figure of Heaven without further calculation, is this–

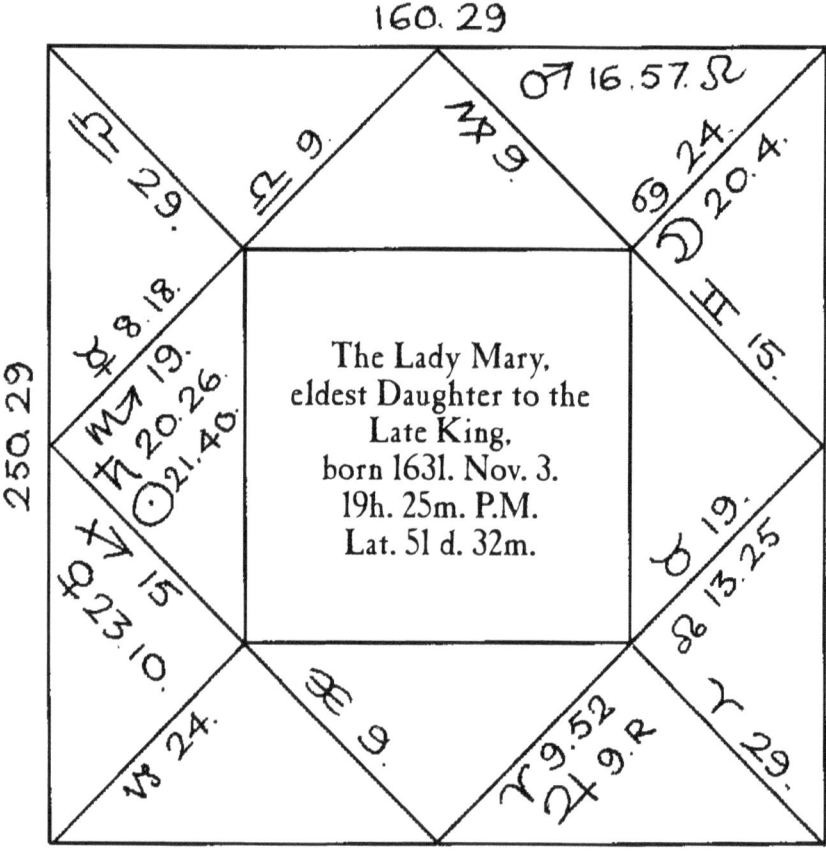

The Princess was exceeding sickly when she was young, as is apparently to be seen from the Figure of her nativity. The Sun and Saturn are in conjunction and locally posited in the Ascendent; and Mars Lord of

Nativity of the Late King Charles

the Ascendent, casts a malitious square unto it, and them also. And most certain, had not the Moon, who is the light of the time, and the strongest planet in the whole scheme, cast her benevolent and friendly trine unto the Ascendent and the Sun and Saturn there, this illustrious Lady had not lived beyond the orbs of her infant years.

The principal accident by which this nativity was rectified is her marriage unto the Prince of Aurange. which nuptials were celebrated in the year 1641 and was occasioned by the Midheaven's direction to the sextile of the Moon, namely:

R.A. of the sextile of Moon	170.	53
R.A. of the *Medium Coeli*	160.	29
Ark of Direction is	10.	24

But besides this direction, the revolution was very pertinent for that purpose also, for the Moon was in conjunction with the Lord of the seventh house, and the Sun and North Node in a prolifical signe; and Venus's radical place was culminating – the Figure itself was perfectly in [trine] to that of the radix.

There is no very great harmony or discord betwixt this nativity and that of the late King her father. That which is remarkable, and chiefly to be taken notice of is, Venus in this nativity is in the very place of the zodiack that she possessed in that geniture, and Jupiter in this nativity, is in trine to the place of the Sun in that. Lastly, Mars who is *Dominus Ascendentis*, Lord of the Ascendent of this geniture, is in trine to the places of Sun, Mercury, Venus, and his own also, in that illustrious nativity. And the greatest argument of evil is the Sun and Saturn here are in square to the Ascendent, and in opposition to the Midheaven of that geniture.

Thus you see that of the two, the arguments of agreement are the most considerable and valuable. Their agreement therefore and sympathy should (proportionably) be the greater. And most true it is that this illustrious Princess was befriended and advantaged by the King her father in the best of ways he was possibly capable of contriving And thus much may serve for the geniture of this eminent Lady.

SECT. 6. The Lady Elizabeth's Nativity

The Lady Elizabeth, second daughter to the late King of England, was born in the year of our Lord 1635, upon the 28 day of December, 11 hours 31minutes *Post Meridiem*.

The place of the Sun to that time is 17degrees 23minutes 5seconds in Capricorn, as appears by the calculation following, from the astronomical tables in my *Doctrine of Nativities Part 2*.

Time given.	Long. Sun.				Apogaeum Sun.			
	S.	D.	M.	S.	S.	D.	M.	S.
1621.	9	20	7	7	3	5	54	24
14.	11	29	36	43			13	16
Decem.	10	29	12	22				52
Die 28.		27	35	53				4
Hor. 11.			27	6				
Min. 31.			1	16				
Lon. Me	9	17	0	27	3	6	8	36
Apog. S.	3	6	8	36				
Anomal.	6	10	51	51				
Aeq; add			22	38				
Ver. Sun L.	9	17	23	5				

	deg.	min.
The R.A. of Sun in that place afores.	288.	51
The R. Ascention of the time given	172.	45
	461.	36
Circle subtract	360.	0
R.A. of the Midheaven remains	101.	36
Add	90.	0
Oblique Asc. of the horoscope	191.	36

The Figure (without further calculation) is as followeth.

Nativity of the Late King Charles

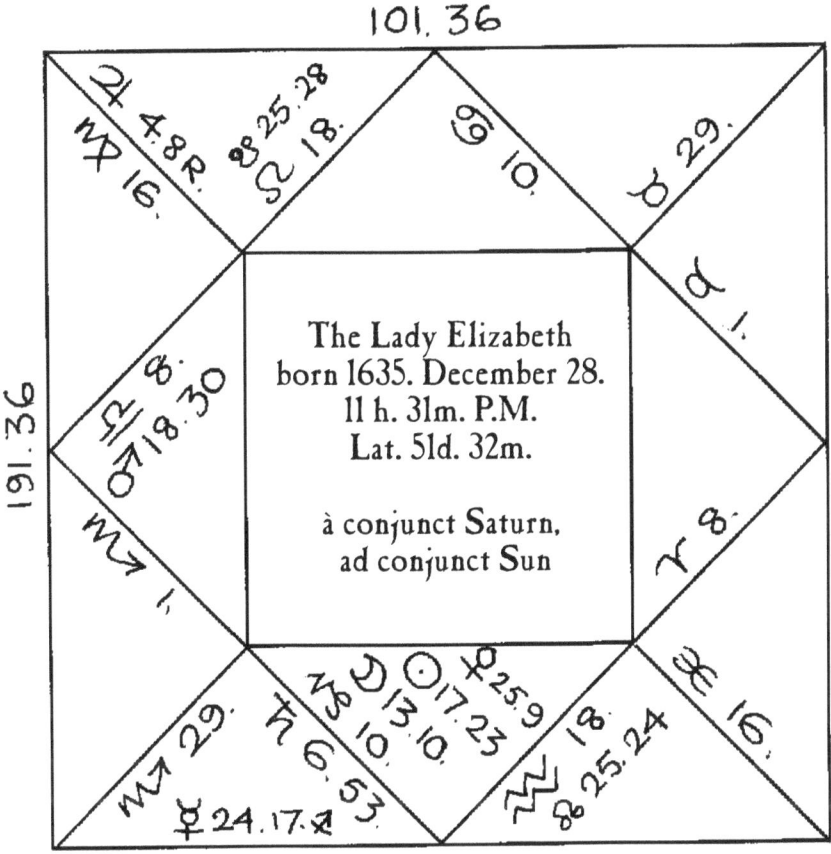

The accidents by which this nativity was rectified were the two following:

First, this native being aged 7 years and somewhat more, had the unhappiness to break her left thigh by a fall; and at the same time, or near thereunto, she was troubled with the jaundies: both which were occasioned by the progress of the Ascendent to the square of the Moon by direction in Libra, an aereal signe, happening within the malevolent orbs of Mars; and in the revolution that year, Saturn was in the sixth of the radix.

	deg.	min.
Asc. *Obliqua* square, Moon, *est*	198.	42
Asc. Obl. Ascendentis	191.	36
Arcus Directionis	7.	6

The second accident of note (as ever I could obtain) that befel this eminent Princess, was that of her death, which happened in the year 1650 upon the eighth day of September. But she was subject to many sicknesses and distempers both of body and mind a year or two before she expired, as was very aptly signified by the Ascendent's occourse to the square of the Sun, upon which direction the dangerous fever first surprised her, (for of a burning fever she dyed). But the direction that proved the cruel *Atropos* to her, was the Ascendent to the body of Mars in Libra his detriment; of which not one native in a thousand escapes.

	deg.	min.
Asc. Obliqua Mars *sine lat. est*	206.	18
Asc. Obliqua Ascendentis, est	191.	36
Arcus Directionis	14.	42

Which ark of direction turned into time, according to the measure allowed by the learned *Valentinus Naybode*, (as I have taught in my *Doctrine of Nativities* at large, fol. 208. Part 1.) declares the time of the accident almost *ad Diem*.

This illustrious Lady was always sickly, from the day of her birth to the day of her death, as may be seen by the position of Mars in the Ascendent in quartile to the luminaries; and Venus, *Domina Ascendentis*, in the fourth house – I might have said to Saturn also, for he is in square to him too – and all these planets are in quartile to the Ascendent likewise. All which positions, according to the opinion of the best Astrologers, are pernicious to health.

But notwithstanding the weaknesses that naturally beset her, she was sufficiently high-spirited, and was also very ingenious, witty, and very aptly apprehensive; as is well denoted by the position of Mars in the Ascendent, and the sextile between him and Mercury, who is posited in the third house of the heavens. Perhaps that later position might make her so curious in her disquisitions after novelties, and ingenious devices and conceits; as most persons naturally are that have Mercury in the third; chiefly if he be in any good configuration with Mars.

Had this Lady but lived to riper years, she would have shared strongly in that superlative and prodigious mischief that the late King her father was subject always unto, namely – the falseness, infidelity and perfidiousness of friends! The South Node is locally in the eleventh house here in her nativity, as it was in that of her father's.

And seriously, considering the many infortunate positions that are to be found in this her geniture, it was little less than a happiness of the first magnitude that the term or period of her years were of no longer date; for it is a truth believed of the religious, as well as asserted by the learned, that it is more happy for a person not to be, than to be miserable and wretchedly infortunate.

There is no great agreement between the nativity of this eminent Princess and that of the late King her father; nor is there any superlative disagreement; for the Moon's place in that is the horoscope or Ascendent in this geniture. But then the place of *Cauda* in that, is the cusp of the Midheaven in this, and the place of Saturn in that nativity is the cusp of the second house in this Lady's radix.

An ordinary artist might have easily discovered (had this illustrious Lady but lived) wherein she should have been a sufferer, and in what she should have proved happy and fortunate, as in either she stood related to the late King her father. But the Lady is dead and I shall therefore spare my further observations on her scheme. What I have done already is intended only for the advantage of artists that are living, or such as may live, when I also shall be laid in the dust. And thus much for this nativity.

SECT. 7. The Lady Henrietta.

Although by much enquiry I have discovered the day of this Lady's birth, yet the hour and minute thereof I could by no means obtain, nor could I produce any accidents considerable to find out the Ascendent thereof, albeit I have used all endeavours therein.

Nevertheless the day oftentimes may and doth do good, as by observing the transits of the fortunate or unfortunate planets over the places of the luminaries, and their own also, etc. Success or misfortune may thereby be discovered, although not in so large a measure as if the true time of birth were known. For I am not of those Astrologers' minds or opinions that (reasonably) allow a transit to be of equal force and power with a direction.

The Lady Henrietta was born at Exeter in England upon June 16 in the year 1644. And the planets places for the noon-tide of that day, by the Ephemerides of David Origanus, are as followeth.

	Long. Planet. deg. min. sec.					Lat. Planet.		
Sun	5	8	41	Cancer				
Saturn	20	2		Aries	Saturn	2	9	S.
Jupiter	20	36		Taurus	Jupiter	1	10	
Mars	29	10		Aries	Mars	1	6	
Venus	18	34		Leo	Mercury	2	8	N.
Mercury	28	36		Cancer	Venus	0	34	S.
Moon	23	32		Pisces	Moon	1	12	
N.Node	10	15		Virgo				

It is very probable before I have perfected my intended *Book of Genitures*, I may procure the hour and minute of this illustrious Lady's birth, (for I am faithfully promised the same); which if I can, for the satisfaction of the ingenious artist and all others, I shall find a place therein for it and present them with it accordingly.

Conclusion.

If any over-curious person, either artist or other, shall quarrel at me for intermeddling with the several genitures of this anciently honourable, yet most unfortunate family; let them know that the art I profess is chiefly demonstrated and made good by the most prodigious and remarkable nativities, let them be either successes or misfortunes. And I find not that any man is interdicted the endeavouring a restauration of that art he professeth, by the most eminent examples or precedents.

Secondly, if any out of an over-precise humour, shall maliciously object – that I have written too favourably of the persons whose nativities I here publish – I answer: That it is manly to speak modestly of our enemies! More especially when they are in an incapacity of retaliating either our words or actions.

The Cedar thunder-strucken to the ground,
Is't fit a shrub, should insult o'er his wound!

And should I, after a malitious and surrilous guise, have bespattered any of the persons (whose nativities I have here presented) with disgraceful epithets, or heaped upon them reproaches and disdain, I had then but vented my own gall, and given liberty to my spleen; and consequently rendered myself more malitious than knowing; and more cruel than Christian; and done neither hurt to the persons concerned in the treatise, or advantaged the worth or justice of the contrary cause.

And although (had I so done) I might in such a case have come off and discharged myself sufficiently to, or before men; yet it would have been a matter of much greater difficulty for a man in the same case to acquit himself to God, who in his Holy Word commands us that we should – Love our enemies, and do good to them that hate us.

Heaven's a Wheel, whose swifter turn relates
In Chequer-work, men's good and evil fates.
The Stars spare none! Both good and bad they strike.
The Low and Lofty, they esteem alike.
Let no man, therefore, triumph o'er his Foe;
His turn, perhaps, is next, to suffer too!

A POST-SCRIPT TO THE READER

Good Reader,

I shall onely desire thy acceptance of this small piece, as the earnest onely of my intended *Book of Genitures*; in which I shall (God permitting me life and liberty) present to thy view,

1. 48 Illustrious or Kingly Genitures.
2. 20 Nativities of eminent Churchmen and Divines.
3. 20 Genitures of eminent Lawyers and Physitians.
4. 34 Nativities of Mathematicians, Astrologers, and Pretenders thereunto.
5. 36 Genitures of Knights and Gentlemen considerable.
6. 50 Nativities of divers kinds.

And what more my good fortune may direct me to the acquaintance of, between this and the publication of that treatise, I shall freely present to publick view, for the honour of Art, the advantage of all that desire to become Artists, and for the satisfaction and conversion of those that in print or otherwise are Oppugners of Astrologie.

FINIS

John Gadbury. 1627-1704

Other Books by The Wessex Astrologer

Patterns of the Past
Karmic Connections
Good Vibrations
The Soulmate Myth
The Book of Why
Judy Hall

The Essentials of Vedic Astrology
Lunar Nodes - Crisis and Redemption
Personal Panchanga and the Five Sources of Light
Komilla Sutton

Astrolocality Astrology
From Here to There
Martin Davis

The Consultation Chart
Introduction to Medical Astrology
Wanda Sellar

The Betz Placidus Table of Houses
Martha Betz

Astrology and Meditation
Greg Bogart

The Book of World Horoscopes
Nicholas Campion

The Moment of Astrology
Geoffrey Cornelius

Life After Grief - An Astrological Guide to Dealing with Loss
AstroGraphology
Darrelyn Gunzburg

The Houses: Temples of the Sky
Deborah Houlding

Through the Looking Glass
The Magic Thread
Richard Idemon

Temperament: Astrology's Forgotten Key
Dorian Geiseler Greenbaum

Astrology, A Place in Chaos
Star and Planet Combinations
Bernadette Brady

Astrology and the Causes of War
Jamie Macphail

Flirting with the Zodiac
Kim Farnell

The Gods of Change
Howard Sasportas

Astrological Roots:
The Hellenistic Legacy
Joseph Crane

The Art of Forecasting
using Solar Returns
Anthony Louis

Horary Astrology Re-Examined
Barbara Dunn

Living LilithM. *Kelley Hunter*

Your Horoscope in Your Hands
Lorna Green

Primary Directions
Martin Gansten

Classical Medical Astrology
Oscar Hofman

The Door Unlocked:
An Astrological Insight into Initiation
*Dolores Ashcroft Nowicki and
Stephanie V. Norris*

Understanding Karmic Complexes:
Evolutionary Astrology and Regression Therapy
Patricia L. Walsh

Planetary Strength
Bob Makransky

All the Sun Goes Round
Reina James

www.wessexastrologer.com

www.ingramcontent.com/pod-product-compliance
Ingram Content Group UK Ltd.
Pitfield, Milton Keynes, MK11 3LW, UK
UKHW022232230426
12048UKWH00016BA/1207